Richard Paul Olson, PhD

Ask Anything
A Pastoral Theology of Inquiry

Pre-publication
REVIEWS,
COMMENTARIES,
EVALUATIONS . . .

"**I**n this fresh work, Olson takes on some of life's thorniest questions and presents Jesus' questions as a powerful dialogue partner. The poignant anecdotes and substantive references speak directly to the contemporary scene. Sophisticated yet utterly accessible and practical, this is a timely resource for pastors, church groups, and anyone seeking to grow in mature relationship with Jesus Christ. Olson has vast experience as a pastor and pastoral counselor, and it shows. This book is sometimes comforting, sometimes challenging, always relevant."

Melissa M. Kelley, PhD
Assistant Professor of Pastoral Care,
Weston Jesuit School of Theology

"**W**hat are the questions that resound within your soul? What will you ask God when your life's journey has reached its heavenly horizon? Richard Paul Olson frames his new book as a theology of pastoral inquiry, weaving together the questions life presses us to present to God with the questions Jesus presents through the frequent gospel interrogations he used as a teaching tool with individuals and crowds. Olson brings to the project a sensitive imagination shaped by countless pastoral encounters with the heights and depths of human experience and informed, insightful scholarship. Every reader will resonate with the interface between universal yearnings to comprehend and the responses God provides in the person and words of Jesus. The book is particularly suited to group study through its inclusion of a discussion guide at the conclusion of each chapter."

Kate Harvey, DMin, MDiv, MEd
Executive Director, Ministers Council,
American Baptist Churches USA

ERRATUM: The incorrect series page was inadvertently printed on page ii; the correct series page appears below. The publisher regrets this error.

THE HAWORTH PASTORAL PRESS®
Pastoral Care, Ministry, and Spirituality
Richard Dayringer, ThD
Senior Editor

CEREMONIES FOR SPIRITUAL HEALING AND GROWTH by Henry Close

ASK ANYTHING: A PASTORAL THEOLOGY OF INQUIRY by Richard P. Olson

TRAINING GUIDE FOR VISITING THE SICK: MORE THAN A SOCIAL CALL by William G. Justice

BECOMING A FORGIVING PERSON: A PASTORAL PERSPECTIVE by Henry Close. "*Becoming A Forgiving Person* is a tender and compelling work that charts differing paths which lead to personal healing through the medium of forgiveness. Close's wisdom of psyche and soul come together in very practical ways through his myriad stories and illustrations." *Virginia Felder, MDiv, ThM, DMin, Licensed Professional Counselor, Licensed Marriage and Family Therapist, Private Practice, Dallas, TX*

TRANSFORMING SHAME: A PASTORAL RESPONSE by Jill L. McNish

A PASTORAL COUNSELOR'S MODEL FOR WELLNESS IN THE WORK-PLACE: PSYCHERGONOMICS by Robert L. Menz. "This text is a must-read for chaplains and pastoral counselors wishing to understand and apply holistic health care to troubled employees, whether they be nurses, physicians, other health care workers, or workers in other industries. This book is filled with practical ideas and tools to help clergy care for the physical, mental, and spiritual needs of employees at the workplace." *Harold G. Koenig, MD, Associate Professor of Psychiatry, Duke University Medical Center; Author,* Chronic Pain: Biomedical and Spiritual Approaches

A THEOLOGY OF PASTORAL PSYCHOTHERAPY: GOD'S PLAY IN SACRED SPACES by Brian W. Grant. "Brian Grant's book is a compassionate and sophisticated synthesis of theology and psychoanalysis. His wise, warm grasp binds a community of healers with the personal qualities, responsibilities, and burdens of the pastoral psychotherapist." *David E. Scharff, MD, Co-Director, International Institute of Object Relations Therapy*

LIFE CYCLE: PSYCHOLOGICAL AND THEOLOGICAL PERCEPTIONS by Richard Dayringer

LOSSES IN LATER LIFE: A NEW WAY OF WALKING WITH GOD, SECOND EDITION by R. Scott Sullender. "Continues to be a timely and helpful book. There is an empathetic tone throughout, even though the book is a bold challenge to grieve for the sake of growth and maturity and faithfulness. . . . An important book." *Herbert Anderson, PhD, Professor of Pastoral Theology, Catholic Theological Union, Chicago, Illinois*

CARING FOR PEOPLE FROM BIRTH TO DEATH edited by James E. Hightower Jr. "An expertly detailed account of the hopes and hazards folks experience at each stage of their lives. Your empathy will be deepened and your care of people will be highly informed." *Wayne E. Oates, PhD, Professor of Psychiatry Emeritus, School of Medicine, University of Louisville, Kentucky*

HIDDEN ADDICTIONS: A PASTORAL RESPONSE TO THE ABUSE OF LEGAL DRUGS by Bridget Clare McKeever. "This text is a must-read for physicians, pastors, nurses, and counselors. It should be required reading in every seminary and Clinical Pastoral Education program." *Martin C. Helldorfer, DMin, Vice President, Mission, Leadership Development and Corporate Culture, Catholic Health Initiatives—Eastern Region, Pennsylvania*

THE EIGHT MASKS OF MEN: A PRACTICAL GUIDE IN SPIRITUAL GROWTH FOR MEN OF THE CHRISTIAN FAITH by Frederick G. Grosse. "Thoroughly grounded in traditional Christian spirituality and thoughtfully aware of the needs of men in our culture. . . . Close attention could make men's groups once again a vital spiritual force in the church." *Eric O. Springsted, PhD, Chaplain and Professor of Philosophy and Religion, Illinois College, Jacksonville, Illinois*

THE HEART OF PASTORAL COUNSELING: HEALING THROUGH RELATIONSHIP, REVISED EDITION by Richard Dayringer. "Richard Dayringer's revised edition of *The Heart of Pastoral Counseling* is a book for every person's pastor and a pastor's every person." *Glen W. Davidson, Professor, New Mexico Highlands University, Las Vegas, New Mexico*

WHEN LIFE MEETS DEATH: STORIES OF DEATH AND DYING, TRUTH AND COURAGE by Thomas W. Shane. "A kaleidoscope of compassionate, artfully tendered pastoral encounters that evoke in the reader a full range of emotions." *The Rev. Dr. James M. Harper, III, Corporate Director of Clinical Pastoral Education, Health Midwest; Director of Pastoral Care, Baptist Medical Center and Research Medical Center, Kansas City, Missouri*

A MEMOIR OF A PASTORAL COUNSELING PRACTICE by Robert L. Menz. "Challenges the reader's belief system. A humorous and abstract book that begs to be read again, and even again." *Richard Dayringer, ThD, Professor and Director, Program in Psychosocial Care, Department of Medical Humanities; Professor and Chief, Division of Behavioral Science, Department of Family and Community Medicine, Southern Illinois University School of Medicine*

Ask Anything
A Pastoral Theology of Inquiry

THE HAWORTH PASTORAL PRESS®
Haworth Series in Chaplaincy
Andrew J. Weaver, Mth, PhD
Editor

Living Faithfully with Disappointment in the Church by J. LeBron McBride

Young Clergy: A Biographical Development Study by Donald Capps

Ministering for Grief, Loss, and Death by Halbert Weidner

Prison Ministry: Hope Behind the Wall by Dennis W. Pierce

A Pastor's Guide to Interpersonal Communication: The Other Six Days by Blake J. Neff

Pastoral Care of Depression: Helping Clients Heal Their Relationship with God by Glendon Moriarty

Pastoral Care with Younger Adults in Long-Term Care by Reverend Jacqueline Sullivan

Ask Anything: A Pastoral Theology of Inquiry by Richard Paul Olson

Ask Anything
A Pastoral Theology of Inquiry

Richard Paul Olson, PhD

The Haworth Pastoral Press®
An Imprint of The Haworth Press, Inc.
New York • London • Oxford

For more information on this book or to order, visit
http://www.haworthpress.com/store/product.asp?sku=5522

or call 1-800-HAWORTH (800-429-6784) in the United States and Canada
or (607) 722-5857 outside the United States and Canada

or contact orders@HaworthPress.com
Published by

The Haworth Pastoral Press®, an imprint of The Haworth Press, Inc., 10 Alice Street, Binghamton, NY 13904-1580.

PUBLISHER'S NOTE
The development, preparation, and publication of this work has been undertaken with great care. However, the Publisher, employees, editors, and agents of The Haworth Press are not responsible for any errors contained herein or for consequences that may ensue from use of materials or information contained in this work. The Haworth Press is committed to the dissemination of ideas and information according to the highest standards of intellectual freedom and the free exchange of ideas. Statements made and opinions expressed in this publication do not necessarily reflect the views of the Publisher, Directors, management, or staff of The Haworth Press, Inc., or an endorsement by them.

Quoted material from *The Shelter of Each Other* by Mary Pipher, PhD, copyright © 1996 by Mary Pipher, PhD. Used by permission of G. P. Putnam's Sons, a division of Penguin Group (USA) Inc.

Quoted material from *Traveling Mercies* by Anne Lamott, copyright © 1999 by Anne Lamott. Used by permission of Pantheon Books, a division of Random House, Inc.

The author has made several unsuccessful attempts to find the source/origin of the following poems: "What Is Success?" and "He Prayed"; and the hymn "Just a Closer Walk." Anyone with information on the sources for this material is asked to contact the publisher.

Cover design by Marylouise E. Doyle

Library of Congress Cataloging-in-Publication Data

Olson, Richard P.
    Ask anything: a pastoral theology of inquiry / Richard Paul Olson.
       p. cm.
    Includes bibliographical references and index.
    ISBN-13: 978-0-7890-2817-4 (hard: alk. paper)
    ISBN-10: 0-7890-2817-4 (hard: alk. paper)
    ISBN-13: 978-0-7890-2818-1 (soft: alk. paper)
    ISBN-10: 0-7890-2818-2 (soft: alk. paper)
1. Christian life—Baptist authors. 2. Jesus Christ—Conversations. 3. Questioning in the Bible. I. Title.

BV4501.3.O47 2006
253—dc22

                                2005018231

Dedicated to Prairie Baptist Church and Central Baptist Seminary
Communities of Inquiry, Openness, and Healing

ABOUT THE AUTHOR

Richard Paul Olson, PhD, is Distinguished Professor of Pastoral Theology at Central Baptist Seminary in Kansas City, Kansas. For nearly forty years, he served as a pastor and church-based pastoral counselor in various areas of the country, as well as counselor for divorce court and an addiction center. He studied with Richard Bolles (author of *What Color is Your Parachute?*) and has provided life-career planning, vocational group, and individual counseling. Dr. Olson is the author or co-author of fourteen books, including *Ministry with Families in Flux*, which was named one of the ten most significant books of 1991 for clergy by the Academy of Parish Clergy.

CONTENTS

Foreword

Dr. Richard Olson—pastor, pastoral counselor, pastoral theology educator—has developed a method of questioning/discernment that draws upon the thought processes of Jesus—and it comes to us in the nick of time!

Shaken by 9/11—and fear-driven responses to it—Americans are unsettled. Basic assumptions are shaken. People are asking themselves, their clergy, their therapists, troubled questions; they want answers.

Long before 9/11 pastor/pastoral counselor Dick Olson had been listening deeply to such questions—and the longing underneath them—and had been recording and studying them with a group of colleagues. In the process of integrating clinical treatment with theological understanding, his team observed that Jesus responded to pleas for healing and understanding with questions—not answers. They then began to apply (be in dialogue) with questions asked by clients and parishioners and the questions of Jesus. They found that when paired with modern questions, Jesus' questions had the same power to illuminate, release energy, resolve inner conflict, and give life as they did centuries ago. This method is so disarmingly simple that one wonders why it's not been widely used before: when folks come wanting answers, respond by sharing the questions asked by Jesus.

It has been common practice to search Scripture for *answers* to questions posed about living a faithful life. Answers based on Scripture can be found in countless books and sermons. They have been codified into rules and ordinances. Often these answers have been useful, providing clear guidance. Sometimes they have been taken out of context and are proof texts for already-held positions. Sometimes the answers given by clergy miss the mark because they do not address the questions asked, or the question under the question, or an answer hidden under a question.

As they intensely studied the over 200 questions asked by Jesus—recorded in the Synoptic Gospels and the Book of John—Dr. Olson and his colleagues discovered that Jesus heard and addressed those whom he met in the deep way. His questions did not avoid an answer. They touched the questioners—who knew that they were understood because Jesus heard their hidden questions and unvoiced answers. His questions opened a path for healing.

I've been wondering why Christian clergy/counselors have taken so long to use Jesus' questions in dialogical healing. After all, rabbis and Zen masters have used the method over the centuries. Perhaps it is because Jesus' open-ended questions about our relationship to God, living the Life of the Way, our responsible relationship to creation and all of God's creatures were turned into answers and into creeds: Being a Christian meant knowing—and believing in—answers. Some religious groups discourage questioning their systems of belief. They confuse the impulse for deeper discernment with doubt.

We also live in the time of *experts*. Today, clergy are supposed to be experts about the soul and religious life just as doctors are experts about the body and scientists are experts about the world of matter, time, and space. Experts are supposed to have answers—and not knowing an answer makes them anxious. We also know that it is hard for some experts to really listen to those who come with questions. They are listening to themselves as they prepare the answers for the questions they believe are being asked.

Dr. Olson's book challenges this notion of expertise. He urges us to develop the "art of not knowing"—the foundation of many spiritual practices. Jesus met those coming to him for answers in an open way. He emptied himself out, did not make assumptions, was available, and did not know the other—*until he knew*. To use Jesus' questions, we must first overcome our anxiety about not knowing answers or about needing to quickly "size up" those coming for counseling. Like Jesus, we need to create an *empty space* for another *to be*.

As I read the book I experienced Dr. Olson speaking to me. Dividing the book into two parts, in one section he probes our human depths with questions asked by others: Where do I find meaning in life? How will I succeed? What can I do to protect my children? How do I know what leaders to trust? What can I do about my battle with depression? What can I do about my burnout and fatigue? The second section probes the divine depths, asking questions: How can I know God loves me? What is prayer? Why is my prayer unanswered? Why suffering? Where do I find hope? What happens when I die? What can I do about the pain of grief?

I have asked myself many of these questions. I can hear Dr. Olson's pastoral voice as he opens up my questions and "sings a duet" with the questions of Jesus. I will use this book for my own reflection, growth, and comfort. I'm taking questions more seriously. I have begun to pay more careful attention to the questions I ask myself, but often gloss over. Because the appendix to this book lists Jesus' questions I have an easy resource for finding His questions that resonate with mine. In listening to this "duet," with the help of the Spirit, an answer, or another question, emerges.

At the end of each chapter Dr. Olson provides processes for personal reflection and group discussion as a tool for individual and group spiritual discernment. I believe that without intending to do so, he has made an important Protestant contribution to the field of spiritual direction (or companioning.)

Obviously, this book is a wonderful resource for clergy, faith communities, retreat leaders, and seekers. It is also valuable for pastoral counselors who "probe human depths," listening to their clients' questions, and who help them use their own religious faith in their healing. Jesus' question: "Do you want to be made whole?" when woven with the questions of our clients, creates a strong rope that can be attached (like that of a mountain climber) to the "Ground of Being." (For illumination of this metaphor, read on!)

Thank you, Dick Olson, for your ability to listen, for your biblical scholarship, for your creative synthesis, and for your insight into Jesus the Counselor. I also want to thank you as a sister American Baptist minister for rooting this work in the Baptist principles of the priesthood of believers and religious liberty. The importance of the freedom to question is falling on hard times. It's reassuring that Jesus is not only "the answer," but that Jesus is "the questioner" as well.

The Reverend Margaret Kornfeld, DMin
Diplomat and Past President,
American Association of Pastoral Counselors
Author, Cultivating Wholeness: A Guide to Care
and Counselor in Faith Communities

Introduction

The quality of a person's life is determined by the quality of questions one asks. So I have been told, and I believe it, wholeheartedly. So, this book is a celebration of questions, an honoring of both question and questioner.

I particularly treasure two sets of questions. I think of these as two strands woven together into a strong and reliable rope, a rope we can offer to one another to help in the frustrations, crises, and tragedies of our lives. I will describe the two strands for you, and then we will use them to consider some of the most basic issues of our life and faith.

Strand One: Our Questions

One strand consists of the honest questions that each of us asks. Sometimes these arise out of our curiosity, our drive to understand and make sense out of things. Sometimes these questions force themselves on us, uninvited and unbidden.

I have been a parish pastor and pastoral counselor for forty years. Time and again, folks have led me—and themselves—to depths and heights and to unexplored territory by the questions they asked. Indeed we went into that new space together as we lived with the questions, explored them, pondered the mystery. We have been strengthened by the power of deep searching questions, openly asked. This is our first strand of the guide rope we will use—our questions, the ones we ask.

We can see the value of this strand from many different angles. For one thing, there is an invitation, "Let's go exploring together. We may be frightened by what we discover. Or we may be amazed. At any rate, it is exciting to go and look." Questions are much more exciting than statements of fact or declarations. They are certainly much more tantalizing than demands or commands (necessary as those are from time to time). Beyond that, questions are a vital and necessary part of a growing faith. John Westerhoff, pioneering religious educator in faith development makes this clear. He points to four stages, or styles, of faith. Although each is worthy and complete in and of itself, there is also a progression, a journey.

The first stage to which he points is "experienced faith." This is the faith a child gains as the child explores, imagines, reacts, creates, imitates, exeriences. In fun, wonder, hugs, the child experiences faith. Putting the infant Jesus in the manger, taking part in a Christmas pageant, joining in a friendship circle around a campfire all occasion "experienced faith." At this point, belief and doctrine are not all that important. (And questions are not necessary.)

Next comes "affiliative faith" the faith of belonging. Worshipping together, being part of a supportive small group, being accepted and affirmed—this, and more, stirs deep affections, loyalty, and being a part of something great. This is the faith of belonging. (The joy of fierce loyalties may mean that questions are ignored, denied, or postponed.) But then, "searching faith" follows "affiliative faith." This style and stage of faith includes doubt, critical judgment, and the need to experiment. At this point, questions are inescapable! Westerhoff notes, "In order to move from an understanding of faith that belongs to the community to an understanding of faith that is our own, we need to *count and question that faith.*"[1]

When "searching faith" has been adequately explored, there comes another stage, "owned faith," in which one's faith and commitment become a central and vital part of one's total being. A person wants to put one's faith into personal and social action, to communicate one's central life commitment in word and deed. At this point, one still has questions, but is willing to live with them and stand on what has been discovered thus far. This brings us back to the subject of the value of questions. Westerhoff contends that to come to the point of "owned faith" we need to experience "searching faith" to doubt, to question, to seek, to experiment. That is the process by which one comes to a profound faith personally held with vital love and deep commitment. At least, for those who have been born into an atmosphere of nominal Christianity, such questioning is one vital way. Many of us move back and forth between "searching faith" and "owned faith," asking, questioning, searching, probing on the way to new convictions strongly held, all of our lives. Such persons are those who make the role of pastor and pastoral counselor so stimulating.

However, this understanding may seem contrary and subversive to the usual way of doing things around some churches. All too often, our faith communities do not value, invite, and encourage questions. Rather than seeing them as a necessary part of the journey, religious leaders may fear that these quests will upset people and destroy the warm, family feeling the church is cultivating. (Some churches, not just individuals, may want to stay at the "affiliative faith" stage and not raise disturbing or uncomfortable issues.)

We need a greater freedom in this regard among us. To be sure, some of us do not seem to need to raise questions about our faith, and some of us are not yet ready to do so. But for others of us, questions express the freedom to explore. Furthermore, there is a feeling of being confined, held down, perhaps even being deceived if we are forbidden this experience. We need the assurance that the teachings of our faith heritage can withstand our most penetrating scrutiny.

So far we have noted that adventure exists in questions themselves, and questions are part of our spiritual growth, yet for many of us a question or two sticks in our throat. We need to wrestle with that particular question long and hard, to go as far as we can, humanly speaking, to find an answer. Or, at least we need to gain perspective and discover a variety of possible responses. We may be stuck at this point and cannot go on until we have lived with this question for a time. Perhaps our dilemma is even more powerful than that. We may even need to *live the question*. For us, it is not simply an exciting or good thing to do; it is what we must do. That freedom to question and the insights that come from such an exploration form one strand in our guide rope on this journey. Certainly, our nation's and culture's experience of the shock and sorrow of the terrorist attacks of September 11, 2001, force upon us deep and troubling questions that we avoid at our peril. I will speak more of this as we proceed. Once we have acknowledged this, there is another aspect to consider. When we ask our questions, for what do we want and expect?

Some of us may hope for a factual, straightforward answer. I smile at a story told by Thomas Long, a professor of homiletics, about a pastor friend. One day, a five-year-old girl, dressed in her Sunday best, came to the church and asked to speak to the pastor. Immediately she asked him, "What will we eat in heaven?" He thought, improvised, and then answered as best he could to a child on the spur of the moment—something like this, "Well, we have earthly bodies and we will have heavenly bodies. We have earthly clothing and we will have heavenly clothing. Now we eat earthly food and then we will eat heavenly food." The little girl left and whispered to the secretary on the way out, "He does not know either." Like that child, we will often be disappointed if we hope for clear, concrete, concise answers to our searching questions. Most questions worth asking don't admit to such clear-cut, easy answers.

Others of us may hope for something less, but ultimately more helpful. Perhaps we want a hearing. It will be good to talk about the question, to walk around it, to say as much as we want about it. We want to know, "Does anyone else wonder or worry about this? Am I alone?" I recall something that my friend Bill said to me in this regard. Bill had come to a discussion-support group that met for several weeks on the topic of "midlife." When it finished, he told me, "I hoped to get answers to a number of my questions. I didn't get those answers, but at least I don't feel so alone with my questions." That is a worthy gift in itself, a gift that I trust I can often give my counselees. We can offer at least that much to one another.

Yet we may hope for much more. We would like to hear some of the more serious attempts to respond to our question. Where does the question lead? What answers, intuitions, or hunches have others who considered this question offered?

On many of these questions, not all the information or wisdom is yet in. It is possible that growth, progress, and discovery can come from our searching. At the same time, we will need to sometimes face that, on many of these questions, all the information will not be in, not during this lifetime, perhaps not during this age.

This will bring us to the point where we realize that for some questions, there are no answers. I smiled again as I read of one such question—again from a child. One day the little son of British philosopher R. G. Collingwood startled his father with the announcement, "I'm going to marry Grandma." Perhaps Collingwood was preoccupied with philosophical thoughts. Possibly, he did not know how to reason with a little boy. At any rate, the best he could respond was, "Well no, you can't do that. It's not allowed." The little boy was irritated and retorted, "Why not? You married my mother. Why can't I marry your mother?"[2] Of course, with a little care and patience, that question could have been answered. Some questions cannot be answered.

Either the place where we are in life, or our frame of reference, or the scope of the question itself may render a particular question unanswerable. Such questions point to a mystery, vast beyond the ability of our limited minds to absorb; and yet, there is health, freedom, and discovery in asking.

Though some of our questions may beg for a satisfying response, though our exploring may feel incomplete, though any answer we find may feel unsatisfying, our open, sturdy questions are one strong strand in our guide rope of this journey of faith.

Strand Two: Jesus' Questions

We raise our deepest questions, collect them, and come to the gospels, the story of Jesus. We come expecting, at least hoping, that he will respond to these interrogations of our hearts.

However, our first response may well be surprise and disappointment. Jesus answers very few of the questions that are closest to our hearts, at least not directly. Rather, he asks far more questions than he answers. In the synoptic gospels (Matthew, Mark, and Luke), approximately 150 different questions are recorded that Jesus asked!

The fourth Gospel, John, sometimes portrays Jesus' conversational style quite differently than do the first three gospel writers. However, John agrees on this. He also portrays Jesus as a questioner. Indeed, John records another fifty questions! So we come to Jesus in the gospels with our questions. Rather than answering them, he presents us with some 200 questions of his own. (I note in advance a liberty I have taken with this information. I am aware of the distinctions between John and the first three Gospels in their interpretations of Jesus. For this exploration I have sometimes combined questions attributed to Jesus from these two varied sources.)

To be sure, the witness of the gospels on Jesus' questions is somewhat mixed. There are incidents in which one gospel writer has Jesus asking a question, and another gospel writer has someone else asking Jesus the same question. Also, passages depict Jesus asking questions and another writer has him making declarative statements on the same subject. Furthermore, Bible translations have slight variations as to what is question and what is statement. There is good reason for these variations, and, uncertainty. The oldest available manuscripts of the Greek New Testament have no punctuation, no divisions for sentences or paragraphs, and not even any space between words. It is up to the translator's skill—and hunches—to detect the questions. New Testament scholar David May feels there may be yet more questions than yet discerned within the gospel texts. For example, he suggests that John 20:17, in which Jesus tells Mary Magdalene, "Do not hold on to me, because I have not yet ascended to the Father" could be a question. Perhaps it should be translated rather, "Have I not ascended to the Father?" With the uncertainties of translation, sentences may be translated as questions and questions translated as sentences. (Within this study, we will follow the lead of the New Revised Standard Version throughout.)

Still, the witness is overwhelming. When Jesus walked on Earth, he asked dozens upon dozens of questions, both with individuals and with crowds, in countless settings, on numerous occasions. He was a person who loved to ask questions and was quite comfortable with questions.

Indeed, Luke (2:46, 49) introduces the postinfant Jesus (at age twelve) "sitting among the teachers, listening to them, and asking them questions." When his mother rebukes this behavior, he responds with two questions, "Why were you searching for me? Did you not know that I must be in my Father's house?"

The adult Jesus used questions as an effective teaching technique. Scholars note his use of the *mashal.* This is a Hebrew noun derived from a verb meaning "to be like." We translate it as a parable and think of it as a story, but it was much more varied than that. A *mashal* could be a fable, figurative saying, pictorial narrative, riddle, hyperbola (exaggeration to make a point), or a proverb. Proverbs and hyperbolas can be stated in question form. Of course, riddles always are! One often finds questions as a part of this teaching repertoire. Questions also occur within the more extended story parables that Jesus told.

At times, he used questions rhetorically (calling for a "yes" "no" or "never" response). He also used questions to introduce a subject. Sometimes, when doing so, he answered his own questions, sometimes not.

Jesus used questions in many other ways:

- He raised questions of those who sought his healing power, or who had already furtively claimed it, and, through the question, added another deeper dimension to their healing.
- He employed questions to confront people who came with demands or requests and led to further reflection and discovery.

- He used questions to draw his followers into deeper understanding, commitment, and discipleship.
- Sometimes he used questions to bring into the open, to sharpen, or clarify a controversy. (For example, a series of such questions about the Sabbath is found in Luke.)
- Occasionally, his questions expressed his human frustration, exasperation, or fatigue.

Questions are also a part of the account of Jesus' suffering, death, and triumph.

- He turned questions back on his accusers and trial judges on the way to the cross.
- On the cross, he raised a piercing question with God. Indeed, throughout his life, he did not hesitate to ask questions of the almighty, ultimate one.
- As the resurrected, living Lord, he asked questions of his awe-struck, still-bewildered followers.

How does this relate to our search? Another little story leads me to one response. A wise man was once asked, "Why do you always answer a question with a question?" Responded the guru, "Why not?"

I connect that story to Jesus the Christ. When he lived his earthly life among us, often people plied him with questions. More often than not he responded with a question himself. It was as if he were saying, "I am not come to be the one who answers all your questions. I am come to be the one who raises questions with you!"

A generation ago, a popular theme for youth rallies was, "Christ is the answer." That theme speaks of an important truth, that life in relationship to and obedience to Christ contains answers to our world's deepest problems, both societal and personal. However, that theme needs to be counterbalanced with another, "Christ is the question and the questioner." His very life as the incarnate-crucified-risen one raises the most basic question with us. That question was never stated more clearly than by Pontius Pilate at Jesus' trial, "Then what shall I do with Jesus who is called the Messiah?" (Mt 27:22). (In the fourth Gospel, Pontius Pilate asks an equally searching question, "What is truth?"[Jn 18:38].) The entire Christ event puts those questions to us.

Within that God-ordained role, he came and asked approximately 200 recorded questions of us. Of course, we know that the gospels provide an extremely brief summary and overview of all he said and did. Certainly he asked many, many more. Could it be that within those questions there is a resource, another strand to the strong guide rope we need on our journey of faith and discovery?

I believe that the questions Jesus asked do indeed provide such a vital resource, a terribly underused resource. We often speak of Jesus as Savior, Lord, Teacher, Guide, Lover, Friend, Healer, and Reconciler. We do not speak of Jesus as Question and Questioner. Yet it is as Lord, Savior, Friend, Teacher, Healer and more that he asks the questions. These questions seem to be the least noticed, analyzed, and interpreted part of what he said and did. I propose we claim this valuable resource and use it as the second strand in the rope we are weaving. There is good news for those of us who value and who need questions. The central person of our faith also valued questions and asked them throughout his earthly life in every conceivable circumstance.

Centuries ago, John Robinson promised pilgrims leaving for the New World that God has more light and truth yet to break forth out of God's holy word. I trust that by being open to this greatly underexplored aspect of Jesus' life and teaching, more light and truth will break forth for us.

Weaving the Strands Together

So we have two sturdy strands—our questions, and Jesus' questions. How do we weave them together? I will tell you what I have been attempting in this regard. The rest of the book will report some of the results of this effort. This process began when I was pastor of Prairie Baptist Church (a suburban American Baptist Church in Kansas City). I began to hear ever-more urgent cries for answers to heartfelt questions about life and faith. At the door after worship someone would say, "Pastor, some day I hope you will preach on. . ." Another person would hand me a well-thought-out note framing a question. Then again, in my counseling office, the hospital, or a funeral home, I would hear yet more questions, often choked out in whispers, accompanied by tears.

I began to collect those questions and reflect on them and asked my pastoral staff to do the same, hoping to respond in some way. The questions most frequently and urgently asked began to take shape.

During a study retreat time, a few of Jesus' questions came to mind, and I wondered if there might be gain in looking at all the questions he asked. I set about compiling and taking notes on every question Jesus asked. For the first three gospels, it was helpful to use *Gospel Parallels*.[3] As the title implies, this resource places each passage in the gospels where there is a parallel passage in another gospel side by side. It makes for easier and more comprehensive discovery on such a topic. I read the gospel of John separately, again with an eye for Jesus' questions.

Then I placed these two sets of questions—Jesus' (as reported in all four gospels) and ours—side by side and asked, "Are there any ways in which these two lists of questions intersect? Is there potential dialogue and conversation between these two groups of questions? If so, which questions and in what manner?"

As I reflected, I began to hear Jesus' questions voiced in many different ways. Sometimes he offered companionship to my perplexity. Other times he asked a similar question on an even deeper plain. Occasionally his questions forced me to look at myself rather than to others or God for answers to my quest. Sometimes his questions pointed beyond the triviality of my query. Instead, his questions indicated much deeper issues that I had avoided with my simplistic questions. Sometimes his questions reminded that an answer to this particular question would not be mine in this mortal existence. At other times his questions were a window to vistas I needed to explore. I never felt condemned for having questions and asking them vigorously. At the same time, I was reminded that we are not to ask these questions just because they are interesting. Rather, the purpose of questioning is deeper discipleship and more comprehensive commitment to that which has been revealed.

For the most part, the recorded spoken questions of Jesus provided interaction and dialogue with our questions. Occasionally, another dynamic occurred. I recalled that Nils Bohr would begin his lecture courses by saying, "Every sentence that I utter should be regarded by you not as an assertion but as a question." New Testament scholar William Herzog II, who quoted this, went on, "To put the matter a bit differently, every assertion is a question in disguise. . ."[4] Herzog was referring to his own fascinating interpretation of Jesus' parables, but it applies to Jesus' life and teachings as well. At times, the way Jesus lived and died, or some aspect of his teaching, proved to be a question in disguise, an implied question.

The immediate outcome of this reflection was a Lenten series of sermons. This search spilled over into small groups, conversations over coffee, personal visits in my office. This was where my process began—in an attempt to be faithful to God and to urgent questions and needs of a congregation I loved.

Both sets of those questions have become a part of me, and so the quest goes on. There has been much ongoing reading, reflection, dialogues with groups of pastoral counseling colleagues and with my pastoral counseling students at Central Baptist Theological Seminary.

This process began and was mostly completed before September 11, 2001. Did that horrifying event change the questions, render some obsolete, raise new ones? No, but the mood in which those questions are asked is now more somber, searching, uneasy. No, but the depth with which the search goes on and the hunger for safety and assurance is deeper and more urgent. These pages aspire to be faithful to the enduring questions and sensitive to the unique times of these particular months and years.

During my local church ministry, I was privileged to be a pastoral counselor, a pastoral caregiver, and the worship leader/preacher in the congregations I served. There is something from each and for each of those disciplines in what I write. I offer this with three groups in mind:

1. My fellow pastoral counselors and other Christian counselors who aspire to care for the whole person. This might be a book they would loan to counselees concerned about these issues.
2. Clergy colleagues as an enrichment both to preaching and pastoral care functions.
3. Individuals or small groups fascinated with or troubled by the questions raised here. For groups, there are discussions at the end of each chapter.

Here it is. We can test the two-strand rope to see if it is strong and reliable in our journey of faith. I once read of a saying of Jesus found on a fragment, not included in any of the canonical gospels. I cannot vouch for its authenticity, but it does have a ring of truth. The saying went like this, "Let not those who seek, cease until they find. And when they find, they will be amazed. And amazed, they will discover the kingdom." May our mutual search lead to amazement and at least a glimpse of the kingdom and our place in it. May it open the way to that vigorous "owned faith" for which our hearts long.

Personal Reflection or Group Discussion

1. In beginning group exercise, introduce the theme "All You Ever Wanted to Know About Faith and Life but Were Afraid to Ask." Have people in groups of three compile lists, and collect a master list from all. Then look at the table of contents of this book. Do the topics there add any questions for you? Are there subjects on that list (in the table of contents) that you would adapt, expand, or rewrite? Make your list of questions as complete as you can.

2. Discover those nearly 200 questions Jesus asked. You might want to do so on your own by reading the gospels (with or without the *Gospel Parallels*). Or, you might want to examine the list of questions the author discovered. It is provided in the appendix to this book.

3. Reflect on your experience with questions, doubts, searching. Has this been a part of your faith journey? Does your experience resonate with John Westerhoff's description provided earlier in this chapter? If so, in what ways has the experience of questioning been helpful to you? In what ways not?

4. Reflect also on what you have been taught—in your family, in church, wherever you encountered this topic—about questions, doubts, searching.

5. What excites you about the investigation the author proposes? What hesitations do you feel?

Part I.
Probing the Human Depths:
A Dialogue Between Our Questions
and Jesus' Questions About Finding
Our Way

Chapter 1

Purpose

Our Question:

Where do I find meaning in life?

Jesus' Questions:

What are you looking for?
How many loaves do you have?
Which . . . was a neighbor to the man who fell into the hands of
*   robbers?*
Why do you call me good?
Are you able to drink the cup . . . and be baptized with the bap-
*   tism . . . ?*
Do you know what I have done . . . ?

Scripture: Jn 1:38, 13:1-20; Mt 15:32-39; Mk 10:17-22, 35-45; Lk 10:36

An eighteen-year-old woman sits at her computer, perplexed. She is trying to fill out her college applications. However, these forms are asking her questions she is not ready to answer, not yet. The questionnaires raise issues as to why she wants to attend this particular college, what will be her major, what are her goals and aspirations. She reflects, "Last week, we were trying to figure out what to do on Saturday night. Now they want to know what I am going to do with my life! And this in a world that seems more uncertain all the time." In desperation, she types out a quick response; "I do not know the answers to these questions. I need your college to help me make these discoveries. I am willing to learn. Please accept me."

A twenty-one-year-old man is driving much slower than usual. He is headed home for the holidays and he dreads the questions he knows will come up. "How are your grades? Do you think you are studying enough? Have you declared a major yet?" At first he loved the excitement, all the parties, fraternity life. His marginal grades put all this in jeopardy, but he cannot seem to change his pattern. He knows he is drinking too much. There doesn't seem to be any future that really excites him. Oh, there are several possibilities, but he hesitates to pick one and say no to the others. (With his poor grades, he couldn't get in most of these fields anyway.) He was shocked when a fraternity brother took his life last month. At the same time, he understands the feelings that could lead to that. Occasionally, he thinks about enlisting in military service, recalling a fairly interesting class when they discussed this. He remembers one of the assignments—he did them that day. A journalist, Chris Hedges had written that,

> The enduring attraction of war is this: Even with its destruction and carnage, it can give us what we long for in life. It can give us purpose, meaning, a reason for living . . . War is an enticing elixir. It gives us a resolve, a cause. It allows us to be noble.[1]

It sounded good at the time, but the present war did not seem to be doing that for anybody. In the meantime, he muddles on, hoping something will happen to make it clearer next semester.

A man and woman in their early thirties have collapsed into chairs in their family room; they are almost too tired to watch the sitcom they used to enjoy. Each finished the day's employment. Then as a team, they picked up the two-year-old and six-month-old children from day care, prepared and served supper, cleaned up, and finally got the children to bed. It is too late for her to go to the church committee meeting she had half promised to attend. Tonight, as usual, they are too fatigued to think. When a bit rested, a question often nags at their consciousness: "What happened to that dream of doing it all—careers, marriage, parenting, and service to the world? Why can we think of nothing now but an uninterrupted night's rest?" They do not want to turn on the evening news—maybe even this harried life is more at risk.

Across the street, another couple, some fifteen years older, has just put out a "for sale" sign. Their children no longer keep them up at night (except to worry about when those kids will come in!). Both members of this two-career marriage have done well, and they are now able to buy that bigger home with a view. They wonder why it does not bring more pleasure. Both are a bit bored and somewhat burned out with their careers, yet both feel their jobs are far too lucrative to quit. Maybe they can enjoy an early retirement with more time for vital interests, but not now, not with the downturn in the economy.

The next street over, another couple is experiencing the perplexities of early retirement. After the party, they had gone on a much-anticipated journey to Europe. Then they had come home to many long-neglected tasks around the home and relaxed rounds of golf. Now what? They do not want to be as busy as they were, but they are ready for something more, something significant. They hope for many healthy years in this new chapter of their lives. What will this chapter be?

In the orthopedic ward of a nearby hospital, an eighty-five-year-old woman leans back and tries to find a comfortable position. Another fall, another broken bone, another round of painful physical therapy. Is there any reason to go through all this suffering again? Or are the good days over? Should she just give up, let go, and die as soon as possible?

All of these people have something in common. They all have questions about the meaning and purpose of their lives. Who has not asked those questions—Why am I here? What makes life worth living? Is there a unique dream/meaning/purpose for my life? If so, what is it?

As we explore these vital questions, we will do two things. First we will consider the story and insights of a person who did so much to help people work on these issues. He helped people find proximate meanings, "meanings of the moment." He did it in the crucible of suffering, pain, and grief. Then we will use those insights to go a step deeper. As persons of faith, we will consider questions Jesus asks of us, questions that point toward the ultimate meaning that beckons us.

First, the story. Viktor Frankl was born in 1905 in Vienna. A brilliant child and youth, he earned medical and psychiatric degrees at a young age. In the early 1930s, he founded counseling clinics in Austria that drew many young people who were disillusioned because, in the Depression, they could find no work. He helped them find meaning, some of it in doing tasks for which there was no pay.

Then came the horrible tragedies of Nazism and World War II. Viktor and his family were seized and thrust into the concentration camps to which Jewish people were sent. There his entire family—siblings, parents, wife, and children—perished (except for one sister).

Isolated and alone, he grimly struggled for survival in a daily battle with death. He and the other prisoners were cut off from their families, fed a daily starvation ration of less than ten ounces of bread and a pint of watery soup. They were given long and cruel backbreaking toil, while dressed in inadequate shoes and ragged, scanty clothing. At night they were put in unheated shacks with wood slabs for sleeping.

In this unspeakable setting, many gave up and died. Others weakened and were executed in gas chambers. Frankl discovered that a person needed two things to survive: some hope for the future, and some reason, purpose, and meaning for which to live.

Frankl lived by these truths and survived the death camps. After the war, he again began to counsel patients and quickly discovered that all people need those two things—hope for the future, and some reason, purpose, and meaning for which to live. Indeed, in postwar Europe and America, he discovered that these qualities were strangely lacking. He believed the central sickness of the time was the haunting suspicion that life had no meaning or purpose.

In response, Frankl created a whole new school of psychiatric thought. He called it *logotherapy*—healing by one's logos—the word for living, or meaning, or purpose. Viktor's message was that our search for meaning is the most basic force in our lives, much more basic than our drives for pleasure, sex, or power, drives which push us. Rather, we are pulled, pulled powerfully, by purpose.

Frankl admitted that not he, nor anyone else, can *give* another person meaning in life. Rather the counselor's task was to stimulate a person in the search for it and also to create the atmosphere in which such a search can take place. However, he added, "But meaning can be found in a much wider range than the sufferer realizes, and it is the task of the therapist to widen the patient's horizon, to expose the patient to the full range of meaningful possibilities."[2] The philosopher Nietzsche once stated that the person who has a *why* to live can bear almost any *how,* and Frankl wholeheartedly agreed.

There is "ultimate meaning" and "meaning of the moment." Ultimate meaning is like walking toward the horizon, one can approach it, but never, in this life anyway, reach it. (We can feel its tug—more on this shortly.)

However, we can discover the meaning of the moment. As we go through life, these meanings of the moment may change, but they are never absent.

These possibilities of meaning are found in at least three broad arenas of values. First are *creative values*—what a person gives to the world with one's work, efforts, and ingenuity. By what you do, you may add to the world's beauty, or the knowledge or welfare of humankind. You may see to it that someone who would have been forgotten has been cared for. Your concern about a problem may wake up the rest of us to this problem. This value is not limited to the highly accomplished individual. Frankl frequently helped persons recognize the creative value of work they had thought was quite common.

Second are *experiential values*—what a person takes from the world in regard to encounters and experiences. When truth, or love, or beauty, or nature touches you, you are experiencing this value. When your mind and heart are stretched by the heroic life of a saintly person, or you have tried on a new idea, or have known something that thrilled your heart that you will remember for a long time—you have known experiential values.

Third are *attitudinal values*—the stand a person takes. When people are confronted by uncontrollable suffering, or national tragedy, or great injustice, or death, either one's own or that of a person one loves, opportunity exists for meaning in the attitude one takes toward these situations. Frankl talked about the "last human freedom," which is the freedom to choose one's attitude toward what life is giving you. If one can meet such events with humor, grace, faith, and hope, then one is embodying the meaningfulness of life in the face of all that would destroy it. Relationships are a place where all of these can be experienced. I can do something for another human being, and/or experience the good things of life with another human being, and/or be deeply influenced by another human being.

These three values, creative, experiential, and attitudinal, provide the broad spectrum of possible sources of meaning in each person's life. They are like three legs of a stool. Lest we tip, we are wise to discover some of our meaning in each of these three arenas.[3]

Frankl pointed out that this is not a religious system. Instead, he used the analogy of a train ride to describe the search for meaning. He pointed out that logotherapy does not provide ultimate answers—final stations. Rather, "It leads patients, the religious as well as the non-religious, to a point where they can find their own transfers to stations beyond, to their own ultimate station."[4] In summary, a statement from Robert Leslie, a pastoral counselor, rings true: "The happiest people in our world are those who have found the life task to which they have been called. And the most unhappy are those who have not even begun the search."[5]

With appreciation for this wise, compassionate, twentieth-century healer, our attention now turns to the founder of our faith, as Jesus explores the ultimate meaning, which beckons to us. In particular, we will consider six of his questions to those first disciples, and to us. The change is not as abrupt as we might imagine, however. For

Frankl's concepts may give us new ears to hear and new ways to appreciate these questions as we ponder their mysteries.

* * *

We first consider a question from the first chapter of John. John the Baptist had pointed to Jesus as the "Lamb of God." In response, two of John's disciples began following Jesus. Jesus turned to them and asked, *"What are you looking for?"* What a powerful, educative question! He knew the answer, even though they could not say it. They were looking for hope; they were looking for someone who could fill that God-shaped vacuum in their life. They were looking for their calling. They knew it and he knew it, but they could not say it. So they simply asked, "Rabbi, where are you staying?" Graciously he responded, "Come and see." They sat down together, talked, ate, got acquainted, asked and answered questions. They experienced love and acceptance, faith and hope. These folks began to see new possibilities for their lives—and for their war-torn world—which they had never seen before. They joined in the adventure to see what they would become and where it would lead. "What are you looking for?"—a question that might open doors or windows for each of the persons of whom we spoke. It is a question about life's deepest hungers, a question about priorities. This question might also start an equally creative process with you and me.

The second question is, *"How many loaves do you have?"* In this well-known story (found in Mt 15 and Mk 8), Jesus speaks to his disciples. He expresses his concern that people have been with him for three days, that they have nothing to eat, that traveling in that state they could become faint. In exasperation, the disciples ask, "Where are we to get enough bread in the desert to feed so great a crowd?" Jesus responds with a question, "How many loaves do you have?" Grudgingly, they responded, "Seven and a few small fish." Jesus took the small gift they had, wonderously fed the crowds, and sent them on their way refreshed and healthy.

There is meaning in the giving, in the doing, no matter how small or how pessimistic we may be about the efficacy of our gift. Light one candle, plant one mustard seed, give what loaves and fish you have, so Jesus taught, and trust the results to God whose resources and lavishness go beyond our imaginations. As we live with our own emptiness and the massive needs of a sick and hurting world, ponder this question, "How many loaves do you have?"

Jesus' third question came after he had been asked a number of testing and probing questions by others such as, "What must I do to inherit eternal life?" and "Who is my neighbor?" Jesus had responded with the story of a person going down from Jerusalem to Jericho, who on that treacherous, winding road was robbed, severely beaten, and left half dead. Two notable religious leaders walked by and left quickly. The next person, from a despised class of people, the Samaritans, stopped, bound up the wounds, took him to an inn, took care of him, and promised to pay more if more help was needed. Then, after the story, his question, *"Which of these three, do you think, was a neighbor to the man who fell into the hands of the robbers?"* (Lk 10:36). Sometimes meaning is found in acting on the compassion one feels within. It may be that purpose is experienced when one is doing the right, responsible thing, whether thinking about it or not. Quite likely, the Samaritan in Jesus' story was not asking, "Am I having a meaningful experience?" Yet the story is told again and again as example to those who are carrying on this search.

The fourth question may puzzle us, *"Why do you call me good?"* Jesus added an explanation of the question, "No one is good but God alone" (Mk 10:18). Jesus said this in response to a young man who came running to him, just as Jesus was setting out on a continued journey. The young man asked a breathless question, the same as in the previous story, but apparently with a more open heart: "Good Teacher, what must I do to inherit eternal life?" Where is the way to a life worth living, a rich meaningful life, a life so good that it endures on this side of the grave and the other?

Jesus' question forcefully reminds him that his is an ultimate question. It needs a vaster frame of reference than his excitement about this interesting new teacher. We are not talking "meaning of the moment" here but rather "ultimate meaning." This can only be explored before almighty God.

Jesus' question was the beginning of the conversation. He went on to take the person's spiritual/moral pulse by speaking of the basic commandments. Then he gave an amazingly direct answer to the man's question about what to do to find rich, meaningful, eternal life. "You lack one thing; go, . . . sell, . . . give, . . . then come follow me."

The person left sorrowfully. He thought he wanted eternal life but discovered he wanted what he had even more.

Jesus' question *"Why do you call me good?"* coupled with his two statements "No one is good but God alone" and "You lack one thing" provide an important clue in our search for meaning. One definition of sin is "anything that comes between a person and God." When Jesus pointed to a lack in this person's life, he was speaking of that which came between him and God. That needed to be given up before he could begin to taste the life full of meaning and eternity for which he longed. The question and the story provide us questions for ourselves in this pursuit. What is coming between me and God's best for me? What is coming between God and me?

Jesus' fifth question carries the search to another arena of meaning. *"Are you able to drink the cup that I drink, or be baptized with the baptism that I am baptized with?"* (Mk 10:38). This comes in response to a request that James and John be given seats on Jesus' right and left in the coming kingdom. (In Mt 20, their mother asks for this favor, in Mk, they request it themselves.) Even though, as Mark tells it, this comes after the third time Jesus has told of his coming persecution they are still thinking of rewards and acclaim. The disciples were so unable to hear these predictions that they did not seem to know that the "cup" Jesus spoke of was the cup of great suffering, or that the "baptism" was the baptism into death. He asked, "Are you able. . . ?" and they glibly responded, "We are able." Jesus' question makes us aware that the road to God's kingdom of love leads through the valley of suffering. It was so for Jesus. He certainly chose that last human freedom of which Frankl spoke. Not only his suffering and dying but also the manner in which he did it holds redemptive possibilities for us. Voluntarily or involuntary, life will ask us questions through suffering and injustice, through pain and grief. Meaning may be found in the way we answer.

This brings us to Jesus' sixth question which came on the last night of his life, at the end of a hard week. Jesus had experienced hostile and unbelieving crowds at times, critical officials, traps and plots, a decision to betray, exhausting days, and on top of that a griping, conflicted group of followers. They were so proud that no one of them would do the gracious host thing and wash the others' feet.

Wearily, aching in every bone of his body, Jesus, "got up from the table, took off his outer robe, and tied a towel around him. Then he poured water into a basin and began to wash the disciples feet." After doing so, he asked, *"Do you know what I have done to you?"* (Jn 13:12).

In their shame and embarrassment, they could not fully answer, nor can we. But in this costly act at the end of a painful week, and as a prologue to an even more sacrificial night and day, we begin to understand.

There is meaning in service and in self-sacrifice. We saw this in so many ways on September 11, 2001, when one of the few bright spots that day was the way so many firefighters, police, and others performed their duties, often at the cost of their own lives. Reflecting on all those who risked so much to rescue, save, direct, guide others, Archbishop of Canterbury Rowan Williams writes,

> It puts a different perspective on heroism for a moment. It tells us that heroism is not always bound up with drama, the sense of a Great Cause, but is something about doing what is necessary for a community's health and security. For most of the time this will be invisible; it is only in crisis that the habits . . . formed over the years emerge to make possible what can only be seen as extraordinary and selfless labours.[6]

If we want purpose in life, perhaps we cannot pick our purpose as we might choose a piece of crystal on an expensive glass shelf. Perhaps the meaning comes at great sacrifice and cost, where the only thing worse would be failing to follow the one who first washed our feet. However much it costs to be faithful is small compared with the one who went before and asks us this question of us. Do we know what he has done? No, but little by little, as it dawns on us, we see the glory and cost of God's ultimate purpose.

We begin our journey of discovery by asking about meaning and purpose in our lives. We discover that we are in the company of many who ask these questions over a lifetime, that a profound twentieth-century thinker encourages and guides this search, and that Jesus invites us into it, on many levels, at every turn. The following chapters explore this question from different angles. For now, we have questions—and possibilities—aplenty!

Personal Reflection or Group Discussion

1. For an opening exercise, invite each person in the group to complete this sentence: "My nomination for the person in the last

century who lived the most meaningful life was _____
because of _____."

2. With which of the persons at the beginning of this chapter did you most closely identify? At what points?

3. Reflect on times in your life when life felt most meaningful. When were those times? What made them so meaningful? What do you conclude from that?

4. Also reflect on times when life felt most empty or meaningless. What made them so? What do you conclude?

5. How would you describe the presence or absence of meaningfulness in your life right now? On what do you base your response?

6. Consider creative, experiential, and attitudinal values. In which of these do you find meaning? In what ways? Which of these do not presently hold any meaning for you?

7. In what ways did the Scripture passages and questions in this chapter speak to your search for meaning?

8. What other Bible passages or questions of Jesus would you add to this discussion?

Chapter 2

Success

Our Question:

How can I succeed?

Jesus' Questions:

Are not two sparrows sold for a penny?
Friend, who set me to be a judge or arbitrator over you?
Don't you know I was also considered a failure?
Don't you know that when you are mine, you cannot fail?

Scripture: Lk 12:4-7, 13-34; Mt 10:29-31

We hear how well the economy is recovering, and we wonder why we are not doing so well. The papers are full of people with lavish salaries—corporate executives, professional athletes and entertainers, university coaches of major sports. At the same time, we hope that our paycheck lasts to the end of the month and that there is no pink slip in the envelope when we open it. We are told of the wealthy elderly, while many older adults struggle to pay for their prescriptions and hope they have enough resources so that they won't be a burden on their children at the end.

There is something strange and upsetting about these days—the most unnerving part is that you and I don't seem to be part of the prosperity some are enjoying.

Whatever that prosperity is, it has not seemed to extend into the job market, at least not all of it. Young adults, especially minority young adults, struggle to get even a toehold. Although there are "help wanted" signs all over, many are for minimum-wage jobs—on which it is very difficult to survive.

People in midcareer are not safe either. Companies are restructuring. For years, companies hired millions of middle management persons. Then, in just a matter of a few years, they fired 2 million of them, because they decided to do things another way. Very good people get caught in these crosscurrents. Carole Hyatt has noted, "*Change,* not fairness, has always been the directional marker that business has chosen to follow. It's a hard truth to face, but it's the way it is."[1] In such changing times, all too often, a grim warning given by Jack Falvey is true. He wrote, "Performance has nothing to do with fate."[2]

An estimated 80,000 people join the ranks of job hunters each day; 12 million people are actively trying to switch to a new career, and 12 million more are thinking about it. When the decision is made by the employer, it is unlikely that the next job will pay as well as the last one.[3] Does losing a job or having a shrinking income make one a failure? What is success? What is failure?

These searching questions extend to the educational, counseling, and pastoral fields. Many teachers despair of a profession they once loved. In their work, they encounter disrespect, actual danger, lack of support, possible lawsuits, and conclude, "This is not what I set out to do." Counselors, who wanted to be present to people's pain, are being squeezed out by preferred provider organizations (PPOs) and health maintainance organizations (HMOs) and other insurance plans so that they can no longer scratch out a living.

Ministers are in great pain as well. Pastoral counselor G. Lloyd Rediger has written a book called *Clergy Killers* about the pain, undeserved attacks, and tremendous stress that surround the profession of ministry.[4] His book is in its fourth printing, and he cannot keep up with the invitations to speak about this all over the country. He has touched a raw nerve in American religion.

As we contend with these personal and financial struggles, a promise is frequently made in our culture. "All will be well"—if only we have the "right" running shoes and a pocket full of credit cards. We are too smart to fall for that, and yet we may be caught up in it enough so that we're barely making it on our current income, and the balance on the credit cards is much too large. Goodness knows what will happen if we get caught in the downdraft of another downsize in this zigzagging economy. Observers note that many people are one or two paychecks from bankruptcy.

Is it any surprise that there is a question frozen by fear in our throats, so that when it comes out, it comes in a hoarse whisper, "How can I succeed? How can I get ahead? How can I even survive?" We still wonder, what is success? It is certainly more than survival, although some days, we'd settle for that. If we are fortunate to have the finances we need, are we successful? Or is that a more elusive goal, measured by something other than material success?

Jesus is no stranger to such fears and questions. However, he offers no easy answers. Instead he asks questions of us that drive us even deeper into our human struggle. At the same time, his questions of us have the promise of perspective and strength. When we ask, "How can I succeed?" Jesus has at least four questions of us.

First, he asks us, *"Are not two sparrows sold for a penny?"* (Mt 10:29). Sold, I guess, to be some sort of cheap, miniscule food supply. In Luke, the question is even stronger. Jesus asks, "Are not five sparrows sold for two pennies?" (Lk 12:6). In other words, not only are sparrows sold very cheap, but also if you buy four, they will throw in a fifth, for free.

He asks that question (are not sparrows a small cost item) and then goes on, "Yet not one of them will fall to the ground apart from your Father" (Mt 10:29).

William Barclay suggests a translation of this verse that is also accurate and even more gentle and sensitive. In Barclay's version, Jesus says, "Are not two sparrows sold for a penny, and *not one of them shall light on the ground without your father's knowledge?"*[5]

Logan Pearsall Smith once wrote, "How can they say my life isn't a success? Have I not for more than sixty years got enough to eat and escaped being eaten?" However, Jesus' conclusion is much more caring. He adds, "So then do not be afraid; you are of more value than many sparrows."

> Said the Robin to the Sparrow,
> "I should really like to know
> Why these anxious human beings
> Rush about and worry so."
> Said the Sparrow to the Robin,
> "Friend, I think that it must be
> That they have no Heavenly Father,
> Such as cares for you and me."[6]

Are not two sparrows sold for a penny? The first question seems to imply, "Let up a little. It takes less than you might have thought, and you have unseen resources to help you succeed." Second, Jesus asks, *"Friend, who set me to be a judge or arbitrator over you?"* (Lk 12:14). This was in reply to a person's urgent request, "Teacher tell my brother to divide the family inheritance with me." He not only responded to the request with this question, he gave them a solemn warning, "Take care! For one's life does not consist in the abundance of possessions." (That verse is a beginning—a definition of what success is not.)

Jesus told an even more solemn story about an apparent success, a person whose land produced so abundantly he had nowhere to put his crops. So the man asked himself a question, and then answered his own question: "What should *I* do for I have no place to store my crops? . . . *I* will do this: *I* will pull down *my* barns and build larger ones, and there *I* will store all *my* grain and *my* goods. And *I* will say to *my* soul, 'Soul, *you* have ample goods laid up for many years, relax, eat, drink, be merry'" (Lk 12:17-19, italics added).

Doesn't it sound good? Doesn't it seem like success as we often think of it? Except for one thing, he only knew two pronouns,—I and my. A child was once asked what parts of speech "my" and "mine" are. The child answered, "Aggressive pronouns."

This man was rather like a woman named Edith of whom it was once said, "Edith lived in a little world, bounded on the north, south, east, and west by Edith."[7] As Cindy Adams once noted, "Success has made failures of many persons."

Jesus' judgment is even more firm. He concludes the story of the prosperous man, "But God said to him, 'You fool! This night your life is being demanded of you. And the things you have prepared, whose will they be?'" (Lk 12:20). As the parable continues, God asks a question with a tragic, obvious answer, "The things I have prepared will be somebody else's." Apparent prosperity is a test of character and this man failed! It begins to appear that prosperity is not, in and of itself, success. It can give one an opportunity to be a success. The questions in this parable lead us to believe that success is more made out of perspective, stewardship, and character.

Contemporary research is providing testimony to the wisdom of this counsel. Ethicist Michael Northcott points out, "Studies of happiness and life satisfaction point to a lack of correlation between affluence and happiness." These studies show that friends, satisfying work, creative leisure, and a rich family life with spouse and children are much more significant. Northcott notes, "The very poor are unhappy in any country," but once basic needs of comfort and economic security are achieved, "increased affluence produces only marginal increases in human happiness or life satisfaction, and may often have as many negative as positive effects on the true sources of human happiness."[8]

Jesus has yet more questions of us; these next two are implied questions.

Third, he asks us, *"Don't you know that I was also considered a failure?"* His mother may have considered him a failure that day he preached in hometown Nazareth and found himself rushed out of town and almost killed! His family probably considered him a failure that time they came for him. They were probably shocked when he did not shut out the others and go to them, but rather told the whole crowd that all who followed were his mother, brothers, and sisters. Many had an expectation of who he would be—he would restore the kingdom of the great David. (Recall the word of Cleopas, "But we had hoped that he was the one to redeem Israel" [Lk 24:21]). Some followers were already planning what part of the kingdom they would run for him. But he didn't climb a throne. He climbed a cross.

A musical review called *For Heaven's Sake,* which was presented to a national youth gathering some years ago, contains a scene that speaks of this. Three men are meeting at a happy hour. One has just been handed a pamphlet that says "Take Christ to work." A second objected, "Isn't that a kick? But he was a flop at thirty-three!" Then they join in a song on that theme: He was a flop at thirty-three!

> His whole career was one of failure and of loss;
> But the thing that's so distressful
> Is He could have been successful,
> But instead of climbing "up," He climbed a cross!
> He was a flop at thirty-three!
> He jumped from carpentry to preaching to the mob
> He just never was adjusted
> So He spent His whole life busted
> And He never got promoted on the job!
> He never saved a single cent,

And Dun and Bradstreet wouldn't list Him on their list;
He could not establish credit
And you might as well be dead at
Thirty-three as have your credit not exist!
He spent His time with fisherfolk,
When there were more important contacts to be made;
He would contemplate a flower
And ignore the cocktail hour.
It's no wonder that he never made the grade!
. . .
Oh, He was licked right from the start,
When He said do to others as you wish they'd do;
For to make it you must drive,
Because of course the fit survive—
You've got to do the others in or they'll do you!
He paid no heed to social codes,
The status factors that can help you get ahead;
Now you and I have never flopped
And yet our names are never dropped
The way they've been dropping His since He's been dead!
We've fought our way up to the top,
We're established men of worth;
So the thing that puzzles me,
Is why that flop at thirty-three
Is called the most successful man to live on earth![9]

Many who once saw him as failure now know that there is no
greater success than to be his follower. Indeed, we are led to recon-
sider what is success, yet again. Perhaps success for us—as for him—
is to be what God calls us to be and to care for the persons God puts in
our lives, whether anyone else notices or not.

This brings us to Jesus' fourth question, also implied. He asks,
"Don't you know that when you are mine, you cannot fail?"

Oh, there may be times when you will not succeed the way you
wish you could, and yes, there will be times of setback, disappointment, and frustration. Our Lord had them, and so will we. But as Peter Marshall, the late minister and senate chaplain once prayed,
"Lord, help us to know that it is better to fail in a cause that will ultimately succeed than to succeed in a cause that will ultimately fail."

Living in the light of these questions and Marshall's prayer, our understanding of what success is becomes ever more clear. Success is to be at peace with oneself, to be a part of God's healing and caring work in the world, to live up to our responsibilities, to love deeply, and to know that one is loved by God from the foundations of the world.

In his book, *The Greatest Generation,* Tom Brokaw tells of visiting France on both the fortieth and fiftieth anniversaries of D day. As he did so, he heard the stories of many persons of that generation, not only during the war but also before and after. He was so moved by those stories that he researched these people even more, not wanting the story of that generation to be lost. This is what he wrote of them:

> At a time in their lives when their days and nights should have been filled with innocent adventure, love, and the lessons of the workaday world, they were fighting in the most primitive conditions possible across the bloodied landscape of France, Belgium, Italy, Austria and the coral islands of the Pacific. They answered the call to save the world from the two most powerful and ruthless military machines ever assembled, instruments of conquest in the hands of fascist maniacs. They faced great odds and a late start, but they did not protest. They succeeded on every front. They won the war; they saved the world. They came home to joyous and short-lived celebrations and immediately began the task of rebuilding their lives and the world they wanted. They married in record numbers and gave birth to another distinctive generation, the Baby Boomers.[10]

Furthermore, as Brokaw notes, the GI bill made education possible for vast numbers of these veterans. In turn, they were pioneers in new science, literature, and art, and they contributed to an economically strong nation. Brokaw's tribute makes us aware that success is also doing one's part in significant groups and movements, responding to the urgent needs of one's times, paying the price of living for one's values, convictions, and call. He hastened to add that the generation of which he wrote was not perfect. It made its own mistakes. Still, he found these extraordinary qualities again and again and wanted them remembered.

All of this does not solve the harsh struggle for survival that is a reality for many. However, we are reminded that there are many ways to succeed. We are also reminded that when we fail, we are in the love, forgiveness, and strength of one who empowers us again and again. "What is success?" an anonymous writer asked and answered beautifully. This is what he or she said. Success is:

> To laugh often and love much;
> To win the respect of intelligent persons and the affection of children;
> To earn the approval of honest critics and endure the betrayal of false friends;
> To appreciate beauty;
> To find the best in others;
> To give of one's self without the slightest thought of return;
> To have accomplished a task, whether it be a healthy child, a rescued soul, a garden patch or a redeemed social condition;
> To have played and laughed with enthusiasm and sung with exaltation;
> To know that even one life has breathed easier because you have lived;
> This is to have succeeded.[11]

Jesus put it even more succinctly: "But strive first for the kingdom of God and its righteousness and all these things will be given to you as well" (Mt 6:33).

We ask, "How do I succeed? How do I get ahead?" He asks us, *"Are not two sparrows sold for a penny?" "Friend, who set me a judge or arbitrator over you?" "Don't you know I was also considered a failure?" "Don't you know that when your are mine, you cannot fail?"*

Personal Reflection or Group Discussion

1. For an opening exercise, invite persons in groups of two or three to recall and tell about times in their lives when they felt like failures, but were really successes.
2. List all the definitions of success that are prevalent in our culture. Also list all the signs or symbols that one is successful.
3. Can you think of definitions of success that have hit home with you? If so, what are they?

4. How would you define success for yourself personally? As a family member?
5. How do the Bible passages—and the questions—cited in this chapter help you in a definition of "true success"?
6. What other questions of Jesus or other Bible passages would you explore to help in an understanding of success?

Chapter 3

Parenting

Our Question:

What can I do to protect my children?

Jesus' Questions:

Why do you see the speck . . . but do not notice the log . . . ?
Is there any among you who, if your child asks for bread will
*   give a stone? Or if the child asks for fish, will give a snake?*
Who are my mother and my brothers and sisters?

Scripture: Mt 7:1-11; Mk 3:31-35

I didn't think it was my imagination—that raising children is more difficult and riskier than it was when I was a child in the rural Midwest of the United States, or even when Mary Ann and I were raising our children in various cities a few decades ago.

In my childhood and youth, there was an occasional shooting, but it was accidental by someone who had not followed the safety instructions adults had tried to instill. Goodness knows there were teenage pregnancies and other reasons to drop out of high school. As a matter of fact, my graduating class was less than one-third the size of our freshman class. Some of the most promising students had left for one reason or another. However, in western South Dakota in the 1950s, there were still opportunities for those who did not finish high school. Then, too, occasional serious or fatal accidents occurred with horses and with cars.

Still, parents had reason to hope that a larger proportion of children would reach healthy, productive, employed, hopefully happy adulthood than seems to be true today. We lived in those charmed years when many childhood diseases had been all but eradicated, and childhood violence had not yet grown to epidemic proportions.

So it does not surprise me that some of the most urgent questions asked of pastors are on the subject of parenting. Some asked straight out, "How can I protect my children?" Others started younger or looked a bit further and asked, "How can I prepare my children for what they will face, growing up in today's world?" Others, knowing of the many pressures asked, "How can I help my children be strong?"

Listen to parents or children and there is fear of the growing violence among the young. Recently, eight school incidents in twenty-four months involved children or adolescents who went on killing rampages against other children. Still, in state after state, the leading causes of death among youths are murder, suicide, and car accidents. The risk is greatest among the poor in inner cities. But the epidemic of violence recently has also come to quiet rural communities and affluent suburbs. Troubled school administrators recognize that the alienation, loneliness, and antagonism among students, and the technology to destroy or maim human life are widespread. The risk is great. Although the murderous school rampages seem to have waned, there is awareness and growing concern about widespread bullying, from early school experiences on. Violence is always a message. We wonder, what is the violence among the young saying, and how can our children be as safe as possible? Now, in addition to our children's expressed rage at peers, is the fear of violence from outside terrorist attacks as well.

Even apart from the fear of violence, succeeding as a child or youth and making it as a family is more difficult than it used to be. The cultural milieu in which families live has changed.

When I grew up, culture affecting my upbringing was mostly local. In a small town, most people knew one another's children and would monitor or discipline one another's children. We did not get away with much! However, our nation became much more urban, and the various mass media grew in power and influence.

Some twenty-five years ago, media pioneer Marshall McLuhan noted:

> The family circle has widened. The whirlpool of information fathered by electronic media . . . far surpasses any possible influence Mom and Dad can now bring to bear. Character is no longer shaped by only two earnest fumbling experts. Now all the world's a sage.[1]

In the intervening years, the impact of such media and mass culture has increased tremendously both in power and negative impact. Mary Pipher, concerned observer of this phenomenon and friend of families notes:

> Our culture is at war with families. Families in America have been invaded by technology, mocked or "kitschified" by the media, isolated by demographic changes, pounded by economic forces and hurt by corporate values. They have been frightened by crime in their neighborhoods. Parents worry about their children's physical safety and children are afraid of strangers. When I speak to or smile at children I don't know, I see fear and doubt in their eyes. I know adults who no longer touch or spend time with children they don't know well. A culture in which children fear adults and adults are uneasy around children is an unhealthy and dangerous place.[2]

She points out that almost every force in our culture works against families. Parents wonder how to protect their children from crime, media, poverty, alcohol, other drugs, and peers with bad influence. It is hard to give a child a childhood. As one parent put it, "Nobody gets a map any more."

The role of parents has changed drastically. Once, good parents tried to introduce their children to the broader culture; now they try to protect their children from the broader culture. Pipher notes "Because of these changes, all of us are off script."[3]

Families are old institutions, but they have new problems. For the first time in 2,000 years, families live in homes without walls—walls in which they can keep their safety and values in, and other influences out. Families find themselves reeling under the pressures of an omnipresent culture beyond their control.

How do parents raise children in the electronic village in which we live? As Bill Moyers put it, "Our children are being raised by appliances."[4] With the ubiquitous TV, children see and hear information that is not appropriate at their age. Before they learn to ride tricycles, they are exposed to sexual and violent materials. Two-year-olds are not ready for sexual scenes or news of the murder of children. Five-year-olds are not ready for programs that show violence as the solution to every problem.

We must remember that all television is educational. It teaches values and behavior. The average child is exposed to 400 ads a day, 4 million in a lifetime. One woman told Dr. Pipher that her son's first words were, "I want." Another mother showed her four-year-old child's drawings of beer signs. Pipher comments that without even knowing it "we are socializing children to be self-centered, impulsive, and addicted."[5]

Economic pressures have required that parents spend more time on earning a livelihood than on raising their children. The strain on single parents, for money, for time with children, multiplies to be almost beyond belief. Thus, while parents may despair over seeing these values in their children, they feel helpless to counter them. Their children seem to be at the mercy of media, child-rearing agencies, and peers who are raised in the same way.

I have drawn this picture with a rather stark brush. Hopefully, not many parents feel quite that harassed. Still, who among us is not concerned with the changes in culture, environment, families, and children? As I lived with these questions about strengthening/preparing/protecting our children, for a time I did not recognize related questions from Jesus.

Statements from Jesus about children abound. He spoke of children in the most positive, concerned, and loving way. "Let the little children come to me; do not stop them; for it is to such as these that the Kingdom of God belongs. . ." "Unless you change and become like children, you will never enter the kingdom of God. . ." "It would be better for you if a millstone were hung around your neck and you were thrown into the sea than for you to cause one of these little ones to stumble"(Mk 10:13-16; Mt 18:1-5; Lk 17:2). There is no question on where Jesus stands. Indeed, his outspoken love for children has been a force in improving their welfare throughout history.

In time, questions from the Gospels did emerge—stimulating queries from quite different contexts. Rather than ask about parenting and children, these questions invite, reassure, and inform. I'll discuss three.

First, Jesus asked, *"Why do you see the speck in your neighbor's eye, but do not notice the log in your own eye?"* (Mt 7:3).

The late Christian philosopher Elton Trueblood recalled that when he read this passage at family devotions, his young son burst out laughing. The child saw how ridiculous, how silly the question is.

That is the kind of question it is, a hyperbole. It does indeed exaggerate so that we will see our behavior in a new perspective. Let us walk with this verse down a number of paths. For one, *"Why do you see the speck in your child's behavior but do not notice the log in your own behavior?"* Recently, there has been great concern about the growth of childhood and teenage smoking. About 3,000 teenagers a day become smokers, and this is filled with many present and future health dangers, including nicotine addiction.[6] The media have proposed questions about how to prevent or reduce this. Almost unnoticed is the common-sense discovery that if fewer adults smoke, fewer children will smoke! Our behavior is the greatest teacher in much of this.

A man paced the floor restlessly, waiting for his teenage daughter to come home from her first date. He tried to comfort himself, "What am I worrying about? Her date is probably about the same as I was at his age." Then he realized that was his fear, that his daughter's date *was* like he was at the same age!

Whatever faith and values we want for our children, we need to begin by claiming that faith and these values for ourselves, and living those out, as consistently as we can.

Or again, *"Why do you see the speck of your child's failings but do not notice the log of your child's virtues and achievements?"*

Some years ago Nick Stinett and John De Frain did a study and wrote a book titled *The Secrets of Strong Families.*[7] They discovered that strong families have several things in common—appreciation, open communication, time together, a commitment to promoting happiness and welfare, spiritual wellness, and ways to cope effectively with stress. They urge a twenty-to-one ratio. Strong families have twenty positive comments for every negative one. Whatever we say to children about what troubles us in their behavior needs to be more than counterbalanced with affirmations of praise and positive regard. Fred Rogers used to do this so well on his TV show, *Mr. Rogers' Neighborhood.* Looking out to the children watching him, Mr. Rogers would say, "You make it a very special day, just by being you."

Furthermore, *"As you think about what is most important in your life, what is the speck and what is the log?"* Is that the way you are structuring your life? Or are you concentrating on the speck and ignoring the log?

This question causes us to reflect not only on the amount of time that we invest in our children, but in what activities we can be truly and deeply present to each other. This is not a new problem. Many years ago, the teenage Brooks Adams, son of Ambassador Charles Francis Adams wrote in his dairy, "Went fishing with my father—the most glorious day of my life." So great was the influence of that one-day's personal experience with his father, that for thirty years afterward he made repeated references in his diary to his memory of that occasion.

Years later, when the father died, the son was going through his papers and discovered that his father also kept a diary. With excitement he looked up that wonderful date to read, "Went fishing with my son. A day wasted."

Although this is not a new problem, it is one of growing urgency. It is estimated that today parents spend 40 percent less time with their children than did parents in the 1950s. Fathers, particularly, are often unavailable; the average father spends less than thirty minutes a week talking to his children. Children have fewer other adults with whom to talk, and so need more time, much more, from their parents. One mother stated, "We're missing the seasons, the sunsets and the stars . . . Our schedules don't protect us. They are stealing our lives."[8]

The strongest driving force in men's movements of today is father hunger. Boys of yesterday did not experience enough father. This father hunger may be even more severe in the men of tomorrow.

Also, originally, the words "grandfather" and "grandmother" did not exclusively mean those related by bloodline to children. The terms simply described older persons who had time for children. Whether we have children or not, whether these children live where we do or not, many of us can offer caring adult experiences to children in our communities. (More on this later).

Furthermore, in this time when many couples are divorced, these families need to find ways to encourage all adults to give something of themselves to their children's lives. May nonresidential parents find ways—whether it's mail, phone, occasional visits, e-mail, or whatever—to let the child know that he or she is loved, and that the child was not responsible for any family breakups. There is another aspect to this question: *When I think of what I want my child to take from this family life, what is log and what is speck? What do I hope my child will most remember and most cherish?*

Often families are quite good at the concrete tasks, e.g., getting people housed, fed, bedded, and transported. They are not so good at the abstract tasks, learning how to manage money, building a philosophy of life, learning how to resist pressure and settle differences, choosing a faith for one's life.

In this question Jesus calls us to address the abstract issues of life—the "logs" that matter. There are many ways to do this. Build rituals with your children. Meal times, bed times, birthdays, holidays, trips, activities in the car, all this and more can become opportunities to discuss what you believe is most important in your life.

Express your faith and values in heartfelt ways such as prayers at meals and bedtimes, devotions, camps, retreats, small groups, faithful worship, and more.

Teach your child how to serve the world. Mary Pipher tells of taking her daughter Sara to San Francisco with her when Sara was twelve. Sara had never seen homeless people before and insisted that her mother give money to every homeless person they met. For a while Mary did so, but then had to refuse because they were running out of money. Sara was upset with her, and Mary promised that when they returned home, mother and daughter would work together in a soup kitchen. She recalls:

> We worked at one [soup kitchen] for a year. We showed up early in the morning, made coffee and passed around donuts and fruit. It was the best thing that happened to Sara during her difficult seventh-grade year. The experience had four main effects: One, it removed her from a shallow and mean-spirited peer culture and allowed her to spend time with people of all ages. Two, it gave her an education about drugs and alcohol. The people at the shelter who used chemicals didn't look cool or sophisticated. They looked sick and messed up.
>
> Three, the work gave her time with adults who were not in a hurry. Homeless people were the first people she'd ever met who had plenty of time for children. No one looked at his/her watch constantly. A woman helped her learn to draw horses. Old men taught her card tricks or told her stories of ranch life in the 1920s. People had time for dominoes, double solitaire, hearts, and pitch. And four, Sara learned that she could make a difference. She could give hungry people food and sad people some

companionship. This saved her from cynicism. Volunteers are happy people.[9]

Remember the question. Emphasize the logs!

We have considered Jesus' first question from many possible angles. Two more questions can further our exploration. If the first was probing and searching, the second is gentle and reassuring. Jesus asked, *"Is there any among you who, if your child asks for bread will give a stone? Or if the child asks for fish, will give a snake?"* (Mt 7:9-10). These are rhetorical questions and call for an "Of course not," response. These are questions from the lesser to the greater—from us as parents to God's care for us as the ultimate Parent. (We will revisit this question in that regard.) Still, there is a clear message for concerned parents here: Stop being so hard on yourself. Recognize how unconditionally you love that child, how willingly you give the child what he or she needs, how you want the best for the child. Trust those parental instincts and urges. Sadly, some of us parents are flawed and cannot give what we wish we could. Even more sad but true is the fact that some parents have had parental generosity squeezed out of them. Tragically, some are unfit to be parents. However, in all liklihood, those asking the questions with which we began are not among them.

Jesus pointed out that, flawed though we are, we know how to give good gifts to our children. Even though we have failed in the past, we can come back to that best parental instinct within us. Trust that and live out the leadership that insight gives you. Take comfort and live with hope.

Jesus' third question was uttered in the midst of a struggle with his own family of origin. Ironically, this question occurred as his mother was trying to protect him. Mary and his brothers and sisters had come to him (fearful that "He has gone out of his mind" [Mk 3:21]). When told "Your mother and brothers and sisters are outside, asking for you," Jesus asked, *"Who are my mother and my brothers and sisters?"* This question seemed to have an obvious answer, but Jesus answered it quite differently than they expected. He pointed to those before him and said, "Here are my mother and my brothers! Whoever does the will of God is my brother and sister and mother." Hearing that must have been a blow to his mother and siblings, but Jesus was not rejecting his family; he was redefining and expanding his family. He led us to see that family is no longer defined by blood or genetics alone. It also includes those who share commitment to Jesus. Jesus adds adoption and foster families to his definition of family, both literally and figuratively. This means that his followers always have a local family and a world-wide family. This is a theme echoed in the rest of the New Testament. Again and again, we are reminded that we are adopted into the family of God, members of God's household.

The promise in Jesus' question needs to be both reclaimed and reframed for our time. Among the many problems parents face, a huge one is isolation—from relatives, extended family, and old friends. If locally available, many of these people might be willing and able to help with the hard decisions and the work of being parents. Though the African saying has been overused, it is still true: "It takes a village to raise a child." But where do mobile parents find a village? It may be found in a local expression of Jesus' family, a church, now that's a village!

As family therapist Mary Pipher wrestles with this isolation dilemma, she recalls a Sioux word—*tiospaye.* It means "the people with whom one lives" and refers to the unit of a tribe that would live, travel, hunt together, and provide for one another. It was also a sort of extended family. Pipher writes, "The tiospaye gives children multiple parents, aunts, uncles and grandparents. It offers children a corrective factor for problems in their nuclear families. If parents are difficult, there are other adults around to soften and diffuse the situation."[10] The title of Pipher's book expressed this basic need of families: *The Shelter of Each Other.*

Jesus' question about who is his family starts us down this road—the road of becoming a shelter of committed friends for one another's families. We are called to help one another in the all-important task of strengthening, preparing, and protecting the children of the community. The "my" children in our original question becomes "our" children. The horizons of the word "our" grow and grow.

I have brought together the wise counsel of concerned family counselors and probing questions of Jesus to respond to urgent parental questions. I hope this has been helpful. However, a further somber, realistic word must be added. There are no guarantees on the protection that parents and others offer children. In a reflection written shortly after September 11, 2001, ethicist Gilbert Meilaender reminded us that we do not have it in our power to make ourselves, or our nation, or those we love absolutely secure. Since there is no complete and ultimate security, he suggests that what we need to confess to our children that this world is indeed a dangerous place. Death is ultimately a certainty, a possibility at any moment. Therefore, we need to explain to our children what we did at their baptism.

> I handed you over to the God who loves you and with whom you are safe in both life and death. There is no security to be found elsewhere. . . . Live with courage, therefore, and, if it must be, do not be afraid to die in the service of what is good and just.[11]

Parenting is a courageous undertaking! To troubled parents, Jesus offers three questions, "Why do you see the speck and ignore the log?" "Is there any among you who would give your child a stone or a snake rather than the wholesome food they want?" "Who is my mother, brothers and sisters?" Undergirding these questions are all his statements of love and concern for children. Finally, his solid assurance, "So it is not the will of your [Parent] in heaven that one of these little ones should be lost" (Mt 18:14).

Personal Thought or Group Discussion

1. As an opening exercise, offer one or more of these statements and invite people to finish them any way they want:
   a. "I feel best about my parenting when . . ."
   b. "I feel worst about my parenting when . . ."
   c. "My most unforgettable memory of my parents is . . ."
2. What comparisons do you observe between raising children now and twenty-five years ago? Fifty years ago?
3. What perils of raising children concern you most?
4. On which issues of being a parent do you feel "off script" as Mary Pipher puts it?
5. What do you most hope that your children will take from your family life?
6. What examples of parenting have you seen that you truly admire? What do you admire about that parenting style?
7. What do the Bible passages say to you about parenting?
8. In what ways is your church or small group already being "family" or *"tiospaye"* or "shelter" for one another's children? What could your church or group do to make this more of a reality?
9. What other questions of Jesus or other Bible passages would you have added to this exploration?

Chapter 4

Trusting Leaders

Our Question:

How can I know what leaders to trust?

Jesus' Questions:

Do you also wish to go away?
Can a blind person guide a blind person?
Are grapes gathered from thorns or figs from thistles?
Why do you call me "Lord, Lord," and do not do what I tell you?

Scripture: Lk 6:37-49; Mt 7:16; Jn 6:67-78

In a "Peanuts" cartoon strip, strong-willed Lucy presents indecisive Charlie Brown with a two-kinds-of-people question. "On a cruise ship," says Lucy, "Some people place their deck chairs to the stern, to see where they have been, and others face forward, to see where they are going. Which way would you set your chair, Charlie Brown?" Charlie . . . has to think for a moment and then he says, "I can't get my chair unfolded."[1]

To tell the truth, I have been trying to get my chair unfolded on a most difficult question asked of us pastors. "How can I know which leaders to trust?" We face that question again and again. Every few months, we are asked to go to the polls and make decisions about some leaders on local, state, or national levels. Do we stick with our own political party or make individual choices? Do we believe those TV ads, many developed and paid for by single-issue interest groups, or do we probe deeper? Democracy is a wonderful thing, and yet, time after time, a leader is defeated for making a heroic, but unpopular stand on some issue, such as race, or gun control, or war, or abortion.

We face that question when we flick the radio dial or surf the television channels. Each week, millions upon millions of Americans listen to rude talk show hosts with their half-truths, untruths, rumors, lies, and total disrespect for leaders in government. As observers of the American scene lament the decline of mutual respect and civility in the way we conduct our lives, talk show hosts lead the way in that decline.

We must also consider that question in religious leadership. Indeed, the original question put to us pastors was about religious leadership. This may be a place where untrustworthy leadership hurts the most. Of all the leaders who should be shaped by ideals and loyal to them, religious leaders are the foremost. However, too often, visible religious leaders have not lived up to this high calling. It's sad enough when prominent religious leaders must confess to fraud or inconsistencies in their lives.

Even more tragically, the twentieth century has given us example after example of religious leaders who touched some spiritual hunger in people, gained their complete, unquestioning loyalty, and then led them into tragically mistaken decisions. Jonestown, Waco, and Heaven's Gate are among recent examples.

Furthermore, all branches of the church are shaking under the impact of betrayed trust in personal moral lives, particularly in regard to sexuality and finances, and efforts to hide that betrayal. In some states, legislation has been introduced to end the sacred confidentiality of the confessional out of a fear that priests will abuse that role. This tragic failure in leadership is not confined to one religious group or denomination.

The question of whom to trust must be asked about religious leadership in local churches—not only clergy, but also lay leaders. In the book *Clergy Killers,* Lloyd Rediger, counselor to pastors and families, writes about the pain in ministry. In that book, he cites these striking statistics: Twenty-three percent of pastors have been fired at least once from a church where they were serving; in 43 percent of those firings, the dismissal was instigated and carried through by less than ten persons in that congregation![2] This stirs some questions about lay leadership. Undoubtedly, sometimes there is reason to dismiss a minister. But one in four? On whatever level, select those you trust to lead you with great care. Always have a questing, inquiring mind about where that leader will take you.

Up to this point I have been encouraging a discerning look at any candidate for leadership. At the same time, there is another side to this issue. I refer to the widespread disillusionment, distrust, and disdain many feel for anyone in leadership. Somehow we need to turn these cynical attitudes around in others and in ourselves. Although some *have failed* the trust of leadership, many have lived up to that trust. So our question is framed in a positive way. How do we also recognize those aspects of character and qualities of leadership that are worthy of stirring our loyalty and commitment? How can we know what leaders to trust?

There is yet more to explore. When we trust a leader and mostly agree with his or her leadership, how do we respond when we differ? Do we need to follow a leader in every detail? Is there a place for loyal opposition, discussion, debate, and discernment?

We must also remember that each of us is a leader in some way. We may lead (or co-lead) a family, a scout troop, a team, a class, a small group, a work group, a church council, a school board, a department or company. When we are seen as leaders, how do each of us live up to that trust? One of the leaders I need to evaluate is me! We need a revolution of trust between leaders and participants in every aspect of our society. Our exploration will not only be about qualities we hope to find in the leaders we encounter. It will also be about leadership qualities to seek and develop in ourselves as worthy leaders.

We bring this set of questions and lay them down before the life of Jesus. As we do so, he makes us aware of two popular ways of evaluating leaders that should be rejected. One questionable way is to look at the numbers. Is the leader popular? Does the leader draw a crowd? Are the numbers following the leader growing fast? Is there a "bandwagon" and is it increasing? Then the leader must be worthy of following. So the popular thinking goes, but there is a half-truth here. We are commanded to evangelize, to reach out, and to draw in those who are looking for a faith and a community. Not only in church but also in many areas of life (politics included), some do this extremely well. Either because of a magnetic personality or a well-designed marketing strategy or both, they quickly draw large numbers of people. Are they the ones to be trusted? Well, perhaps yes, perhaps no.

We need only to look at Jesus to realize how untrustworthy evaluating by numbers is. He drew crowds when he fed and healed. He lost the crowds when he confronted them with the depth, costliness, sacrifice, and scandal of his teaching. After his teaching offended, huge crowds forsook him, saying, "This teaching is difficult; who can accept it?" He then raised a piercing question with the small group of remaining disciples *Do you also wish to go away?* Simon Peter had a much better way of evaluating his leader than numbers. He responded, "Lord, to whom can we go? You have the words of eternal life" (Jn 6:60, 67-68).

Recall also that on the day Jesus died, he was down to a few women disciples and one of the original twelve. Yet this is the leader who, throughout history has been the one to whom we turn again and again. We will need something else than numbers to make a decision.

Another way leaders are evaluated is by appearance and style. In this era of such large media exposure, we expect the leader to be attractive and winsome and to deliver his or her message flawlessly. When that happens, many do not need much more and will follow. Style triumphs over substance these days. Pick the handsome, beautiful, media-savvy person. However, if you trust in that too much, you are a sitting duck for unworthy leadership! I recently read a statistic (in a book on preaching) that shocked me. In evaluating a speaker these days, people rely 93 percent on style, and 7 percent on content. As I reflect, I should not be surprised by that discovery. Over and over again, I hear the comment about a speaker, "Wasn't that wonderful! The speaker was so sincere, spoke from the heart, and didn't use a single note!" That is entirely an evaluation on style. There is absolutely no evaluation of the content, or of the worthiness of what the person said.

Recently I watched an interview with Walter Cronkite, pioneering and highly respected news commentator. The interviewer mentioned that in Cronkite's years as a news analyst, he had been frequently mentioned as a possible candidate for political office. Had he been invited to run for public office, and was he tempted to do so? Cronkite responded that on a number of occasions he had been urged to run by someone who promised to back him. These invitations ranged from senator to president of the United States. Then Walter went on to say that the thing that distressed him was that none of these potential backers ever asked him what he believed, what he stood for. They simply said he would be easily electable because he was so well-known. When we are too strongly influenced by appearance and style, we need to hear an implied question from Jesus. "Do you not know I would have flunked the appearance test? I came to fulfill the words of the prophet Isaiah who wrote, 'he had no form or majesty that we should look at him nothing in his appearance that we should desire him'" (Is 53:2b).

Nor would have Jesus' great follower, Paul, made it on the attractiveness scale. He acknowledged that his opponents said of him, "His letters are weighty and strong, but his bodily presence is weak, and his speech contemptible" (II Cor 10:10). Numbers/popularity and attractiveness/image are insufficient guides in evaluating a leader.

If those are inadequate guidelines, what else will help us to discern the true and faithful leaders and follow aright? The questions Jesus raises in Luke 6:37-49 can guide us here. Along with helpful commentary, are a series of penetrating questions: *"Can a blind person guide a blind person?" Why do you call me 'Lord, Lord,' and do not do what I tell you?"*

Jesus offers us ways to evaluate our own faithfulness and commitment and therefore our own leadership, one of our pursuits. These in turn help us to evaluate any possible leader as well as that leader's teaching or direction. We need to do both at the same time, look at ourselves and look at those out front. Jesus gives us several things to consider.

1. *Look at the person's eyesight.* "Can a blind person guide a blind person?" Is this person blind to truths that are important to you and to basic Christian teaching? Does this person give any evidence of having spent the time and paid the price to be worthy to lead in the issue under concern? Is this person blind to flaws in himself or herself that he or she seeks to correct in others? How well does the person see the road on which we will be led? How well does the person see himself or herself?

2. *Look at the person's life.* In Luke 6:40, Jesus says something extremely striking: "A disciple is not above the teacher, but everyone who is fully qualified will be like [the] teacher." I need to ask this question both as a follower and as a leader. As I look at this person, the quality of that person's life, do I deeply and truly desire to be like the leader, "fully qualified to be like my teacher?" If I teach or lead, will I be willing for my students to come out just like me? Every person is different of course, but in the essential qualities I am communicating, is it okay if they totally embrace, not only what I teach, but also what I am?

3. *Check their fruits.* ". . . it is out of the abundance of the heart that the mouth speaks," Jesus says. In a parallel passage (Mt 7:16), Jesus asks, *"Are grapes gathered from thorns or figs from thistles?"*

Look at the fruit of a person's life or an organization's life. Fruit takes a whole season to be ready. The budding of the trees, the flowers, the forming of green fruit, and its gradual ripening must occur. In all this, the tree will need to endure all kinds of weather, including storms that will tear away its branches and possibly destroy its fruit.

One way to check the fruit is to give the leader or organization time. Watch the person or group through a season, a year, a decade, or a generation. For many new, dynamic, fast-growing groups, the real test will be when the torch is passed on to the next generation. Will the zest and vitality survive? We do not always have that much time to decide about a group's worthiness, but it is okay to question and wonder.

Check not only the development over time but also the outcomes of what the person or group is saying and doing. Are their results consistent with what they say they stand for, "No good tree bears bad fruit, nor again does a bad tree bear good fruit; for each tree is known by its own fruit" (Lk 6:43). Again, *"Are grapes gathered from thorns or figs from thistles?"*

4. *Investigate the foundations.* Have they dug deeply and built their foundation on a rock, or are they building without foundations? Does this leader or group claim new discovery without reference to what has been learned in history about this subject? The saying is true that those who ignore history are doomed to repeat its errors.

Does the leader strike out for himself or herself without contact and scrutiny from kindred Christian groups? Have they done their homework, explored history and precedents, made connections, and then gone on beyond that? Or are they a sloppily assembled organization reinventing wheels that do not need to be reinvented, ignoring history and indeed repeating its errors?

Does the leader give evidence of having meditated upon, pondered, and claimed the foundational teachings of the faith he or she proclaims? Have they made it their own, thus able to communicate it in a fresh and compelling way? Jesus' word about firm foundations means much more than that, but it at least means this much.

5. *Look for consistency or inconsistency.* Jesus asks our leaders and us, *"Why do you call me 'Lord, Lord,' and do not do what I tell you?"*

Part of the consistency we seek is balance. Most of the heresies that have happened in Christian history occurred because someone became so enthused about one aspect of Christian truth that they emphasized it without keeping it in balance with other Christian teachings. Is the stance of this leader consistent with the whole of Christian teaching? Is the emphasis kept in appropriate tension with other doctrines and beliefs? Again, this is a difficult question, but it is one worth asking.

Another basic part of consistency is the balance between "saying" and "doing," between teaching and attitude and method, between "talking the talk" and "walking the walk." In his book *Stealing Jesus*[3] Bruce Bawer contends that certain kinds of Christianity ignore Jesus' teaching and embodying a life of love, reaching out to people in all circumstances of life. Rather, they substitute a narrow judgmentalism that excludes those who do not believe the same way.[3] Bawer makes a compelling case. Of course, most of us see the shortcomings in others more quickly than we see them in ourselves. Still, in this world, where many compete for our loyalty and followership, we need some standards, some perspectives to help us choose.

In the end, each of us needs to ask ourselves and others—are we consistent? Do we both call Jesus "Lord," *and* do the things he tells us?

Knowing what leaders to follow will always be a mystery. Becoming worthy leaders is a lifelong pursuit. Still, there is basic, sound guidance in the Scripture we have considered. We are told not to be overwhelmed by the evidence of numbers or style. We are told to check these things about a leader: eyesight; willingness and worthiness to be imitated; fruit; foundations; and above all, consistency. There is much to ponder in our leader's question, *"Why do you call me 'Lord, Lord,' and do not do the things I tell you?"*

Personal Thought or Group Discussion

1. For an opening exercise, spend some time remembering leaders—from local to national to world, in all areas of your life—who lived up to your trust. What were the qualities that led you to follow and keep following? Make a list of the leaders named and the qualities mentioned. If people have a hard time recalling any such leaders, what is to be learned from that difficulty?

2. Also, spend some time remembering leaders—again in all aspects of life—who disappointed you and lost you as an admirer or follower. What brought about the change?

3. Do you agree with the contention that people today are overly influenced by numbers (popularity) and appearance (image)? If so, what suggestions do you have for counteracting these undue influences?

4. Look at yourself as a leader. About which qualities do you rejoice? In what areas is there room for growth?

5. How did the Scripture passages, in particular Luke 6:37-49, help provide guidelines for assessing potential leaders in your life?

6. What other questions of Jesus or what other Scripture passages do you find helpful in pondering the question "How do I know what leaders to trust?"

Chapter 5

Depression

Our Question:

What can I do about my battle with depression?

Jesus' Questions:

Has no one condemned you?
Do you love me?

Scripture: Jn 8:1-11, 21:15-25

I am lost in an immense underground cavern with tangled, unending passages. What distant light I could once see soon shrinks to a glimmer and now is gone. Earlier I tried mightily to get out, to find the light of day again, but it is no longer possible and I no longer care. I'm very, very tired.

I don't have energy to turn back, to find my way out. It would be futile anyway. I have no real hope for the direction I am going. There is no real reason to continue, but I am afraid to stop; I might never move again.

I am very cold. My hands are numbed by the cold, scarred and caked with blood from my falls on the dark uneven floor.

People (those who wish me well and those who don't) are irritants. They want something from me, or they want to do something for me (which I do not want). . . . There is nothing I want to do. Nothing excites me. . .

Why should I go on? I see no light, no end, no way out. No one beckons me. All that exist are cold, damp walls closing in on me. Ahead is a useless journey, exhausted step following exhausted step, leading deeper into the unknown. Why not throw myself on the ground and let numbed sleep peacefully overcome? I blunder on.[1]

These words were written by Howard Stone, one of the leading pro-
fessors of pastoral counseling in our country. He penned them late at
night in the midst of a long-term encounter with depression when the
cavern he mentioned was so vivid, that the bedroom where he wrote
them was a blur. He tells us what was going on:

> I was depressed. I had been so for several months and had sev-
> eral more to look forward to. I was not greatly incapacitated. I
> functioned in my job, gave service to the community, visited my
> friends, stayed married. But there was little joy. The images and
> the despair of that cavern dominated my inner world for a long
> time. I was one of the six million people in the United States
> who, at any given time, are depressed.[2]

A question pastors are often asked is this, "What can I do about this
sadness that won't leave me, this aching, this void inside?" For every
person who asks it, there are many others feeling it but not asking.
They may not have the energy to inquire, or may assume that's the
way life is. Mental health professional Richard O'Connor believes,
"We are living in an epidemic of depression. Every indication suggests that more people are depressed, more of the time, more severely, and starting earlier than ever before."[3] For years, depression
has been considered the "common cold" of mental health problems,
consuming about 20 percent of the time and attention at mental health
clinics. It seems to be getting more problematic, not only in yours and
my experience but also across society.

Consider this information:

- Approximately 20 million Americans will experience an episode of major depression in their lifetimes. This includes children, youths, adults, and older adults.
- The estimated cost to society from this disease is 44 billion dol-
  lars a year, second only to cancer, and approximately the same
  as the cost of heart disease or of AIDS.
- Studies show that for each successive generation, depression is
  likely to begin at earlier ages, and that over the course of a lifetime, the risk of depression keeps increasing.
- An estimated 6 million elderly persons suffer from some form
  of depression, but three-quarters of these cases are unrecog-

nized, undiagnosed, and undertreated, despite regular medical care.

- Twenty-five percent of all women and 11.5 percent of all men will have a depressive episode at least once in their lives. However, this reported lower incidence among men may really be a mistake arising from the way we diagnose. Men are socially prohibited from expressing or even experiencing (or even recognizing) the feelings associated with depression. Instead, they act them out through substance abuse, violence, and self-destructive behavior.
- Depression has been an issue in the lives of some famous people who accomplished important things. Among them are Abraham Lincoln, Winston Churchill, Eleanor Roosevelt, and Sigmund Freud.

"Depression is a disease both of the mind and of the body, the present and the past. . . . The hallmark of depression is a persistent sad or 'empty' mood, sometimes experienced as tension or anxiety. Life lacks pleasure."[4] It affects emotions, they are usually sad, marked by pain, sighing, and tears. It affects physical activity, which usually slows down, perhaps affects appetite and sleep, one way or the other. It affects thought processes; much of one's thinking becomes negative and pessimistic.

Following are at least three common types of depression:

1. *Major depression:* Often triggered by a severe loss, crisis, or change.
2. *Dysthymia:* An enduring, long-lasting, low-grade depression, so long that a person may forget what it's like to feel good; a person is prevented from living up to his or her potential.
3. *Manic-depressive illness:* Also called *bipolar disorder,* in which a person alternates between periods of depression and of hyper-activity and attitude.[5]

People living with this illness in its various forms are fighting a brave battle. I wholeheartedly agree with Dr. E. Fuller Torrey who writes,

When the history of [mental illness] is finally written—after its component brain diseases have been sorted out and successfully treated, there will be a chapter of HEROES. Foremost will be the PA-

TIENTS themselves who suffered the terrible ordeal. . . . Just behind them, however, will come the FAMILIES who had to pick up shattered dreams and carry on bravely. In twentieth century literature there will be few groups who will match the courage . . . of THESE.[6]

A spiritual component is involved in this struggle. Christian mystics spoke of "the dark night of the soul," an extended time of spiritual dryness when nothing seems to afford hope and light. Job spoke of this. In the book that bears his name, he cries out,

> For the arrows of the Almighty are in me; my spirit drinks their poison. . . . My eye has grown dim from grief, and all my members are like a shadow. . . . My days are past, my plans are broken off, the desires of my heart. (Job 6:4, 17:7, and 11)

Or as in the 69th Psalm:

> Save me, O God, for the waters have come up to my neck.
> I sink in deep mire where there is no foothold;
> I have come into deep waters, and the flood sweeps over me.
> I am weary with my crying; my throat is parched.
> My eyes grow dim with waiting for my God. (Psalm 69:1-3)

What causes this battle with depression in many of us? No one knows why some of us are more prone to depression than others. It appears that one or more of several factors may be involved, including biochemical reasons. Shortages or imbalances of mood-influencing chemicals in the brain may play a part. There may be genetic patterns inherent in some of these depressive illnesses. Certainly, personality type plays a part—persons who are perfectionistic, self-critical, or self-demanding tend to suffer more. Of course, one can live in depression-promoting environments, negative, critical, demanding, conflicted situations.

Very often, some harsh life situation triggers this illness. A frequent cause is unresolved grief. We are left bereft by the loss of someone very important in our life. Grief from friends moving away or from divorce may figure in. Or perhaps a person is overwhelmed with a guilt that he or she does not want to confess and fears God will not forgive. Or, persons may have tremendous rage or anger that they will not express. It may be anger toward an individual, or it may be over injustice in society or in the way we feel we were treated by God.

I've suffered two long-term depressive episodes myself. One came after my fortieth birthday. I suppose it was a classic midlife crisis. For months on end, I either dreamt about death every night, or my first thought in the morning was on the shortness of life and my coming death. The whole world looked dark, dim, and without joy. I struggled to go on. My experience was much like the one Howard Stone described at the beginning of this chapter.

The other came while I was grieving my mother's death. In retrospect, I did not give myself enough time to be apart, do the necessary grief work, and heal. Instead I returned to a tense time in the life of the church I then served. At the time, a series of listening meetings to identify the church's problems and possible solutions were taking place. It seemed, to me at least, that all of that church's shortcomings fell on my shoulders. I felt unjustly blamed for problems that were beyond my control. That was at a time when I felt least able to accept blame, or even responsibility. As with Howard Stone's experience, people seemed only to be irritants, the whole world bleak and without hope. I can still feel the pain even as I write these words. With both of these episodes, my depression gradually lifted as I received counseling, exercised, talked with friends, prayed, and meditated.

By whatever means, sooner or later, many of us come to this physical-emotional-spiritual disease called depression. Author William Styron, a veteran of bouts with depression, once said that the word depression is "a true wimp of a word for such a major illness."[7] He would rather use the word, "storm—a veritable howling tempest in the brain," as a closer description. Those who have been there will likely agree.

The good news is that depression is one of the most treatable of all mental health maladies. It is estimated that 90 percent can be cured, or at least considerably improved with the right collection of treatment options. This might include a combination of medications, good counseling, the learning of new life habits such as sleeping, eating, and in particular, exercise.

A vital part of dealing with depression is learning new ways of praying. Too often people do not feel free to speak before God of the very things that bring depression to them. If you have trouble telling God what is troubling, start by praying the Psalms. Many of them include loud depressed cries including anger with God at God's injustice (as perceived by the Psalmist).

In addition, it is good to learn new ways of meditating. A basic method is this: be quiet and concentrate on just one word that expresses something of God's resources for you. It might be love, grace, peace, shepherd. Just be quiet with God, repeating that one word you have selected. Say the word—inwardly or aloud—with every breath. Try this simple style of meditating for five to ten minutes.

If you are struggling with this sad aching void inside, I also urge you to seek the best of medical and counseling assistance, including spiritual counsel. If you don't know where to turn, very likely your pastor can help you locate such services.

As an important part of seeking that help, turn to your faith and to your Lord. For Jesus is no stranger to our feelings. Indeed, he responded to folks struggling with these very issues, and we find the accounts on Gospel pages. Consider two such incidents.

In John 8, we see a woman who has every reason to be depressed. She is being used as a pawn in a battle between religious authorities and Jesus. This poor soul is at risk for her life, for the law does indeed decree that adulterers should be stoned. She may feel guilty for what she has done, or she may be beyond guilt for doing one of the few things a woman alone could do to provide for her dependents. Certainly, she feels shame as the object of all these judging and voyeuristic eyes. She smarts under the injustice of it all. It takes two people to engage in sexual joining. Where is the partner? Why did they let her partner go free and bring only her to this public trial and ridicule? They come with their pointed, trapping questions. Jesus silently kneels down and writes with his finger on the ground before him. I wonder what he writes. Perhaps it is, "Love the Lord your God and your neighbor as yourself." He keeps his silence, perhaps hoping they will hear their own rude, harsh voices and go away. But they do not. They keep asking, persisting, pushing. Finally, he stands up, looks them straight in the eye, and answers, "Stone her if you must. Let anyone among you who is without sin be the first to throw a stone at her."

One by one, starting with the elders, they go away until Jesus is alone with the woman. Finally Jesus speaks to her, *"Woman, where are they? Has no one condemned you?"* "No one, sir," she responds. Jesus speaks again, "Neither do I condemn you. Go your way, and from now on do not sin again."

End of story.

I wish there were a sequel and that we knew what happened next. I would imagine that when that woman went to her dwelling, she had something new to consider. In this harsh world, filled with people that would use and abuse her, there was one who loved her unconditionally, and—at least that day—he had the last word. I would wager that truth changed her life, and the way she felt about herself as well. Not only was she alive when she could as well have been dead, she had new reason for living. Is it too much to speculate that she felt her depression beginning to lift?

The other Scripture passage (John 21:15-23) is the very last post-resurrection conversation that John records. The disciples have gone back to Galilee, gone back to fishing, and have caught nothing. The risen Christ mysteriously calls out to them, helps them with a catch, and prepares them breakfast.

When they finish breakfast, Jesus and Peter go for a little walk. They sit down on a rock by the sea, for they both know they have things to talk about. Peter expects a reprimand, which he will take like a man. He is full of guilt at his failure and denial of Jesus. He is embarrassed and ashamed to meet the one he's failed. He is sure that he is busted, through, washed up. So, he has gone back to where he was when he started, back to fishing. But how can he go back after such experiences as he has had? He does not fit anywhere anymore. He is depressed and ashamed. When they finally can have that talk, what Jesus says is quite different from what Peter expects. Jesus simply asks him a question: *"Simon, son of John, do you love me more than these?"* There is an ambiguity in this question. Jesus may gesture to the boats and nets, and ask, "Simon, do you love me more than your stuff, than fishing, than your original career?" Or Jesus may nod to the other disciples, "Simon, you once boasted that even if the others fled, you would not. Can you make that claim once more, *do you love me* more than these?" (or Jesus may mean both).

He replies, "Yes, Lord, you know I love you." Jesus responds "Feed my lambs. Do what I've always asked you to do. You are far from busted. Rather you are placed in the role that I once filled for you—that of shepherd."

Jesus asks three times. "Simon, do you love me? Do you mean it? Do you really mean it? Do you really, really mean it? Will you affirm your love as many times as you failed?" When Simon responds, each time Jesus tells him to be shepherd. Depressed persons need people who care. They need people who will not be turned off by their down moods. They need small steps, important, manageable tasks. The risen Christ gives Petrer all that and more—Jesus also promises a powerful presence with Peter through all his future triumphs and failures.

A remarkable human touch is present in John's account at this point. Sometimes a sign that depression is lifting is an expression of anger or contrariness. It is so with Peter. Having just received this assurance and commission, he looks over and sees another disciple, one of his competitors for Jesus' trust and affection. Peter asks, "What about him?" In essence, Jesus responds, "Peter, your and my plate is full enough, let's leave it that." Actually, Jesus' response is one more question, *"What is that to you?"* They were in a new era, but some things would never change. With that bit of repartee, John's Gospel closes. The rest of the New Testament reveals the information that Peter's depression was gone. He would keep the promise he made with power and authority!

Those two Scripture passages can comfort anyone with sadness and depression inside. They remind us that along with turning to the best of the medical and mental health help available today, we have another resource. This is absolutely basic to our well-being.

That resource is a loving Savior who restored, renewed, and challenged people regardless of past failures, in spite of guilt and shame. He embraced them with all their conflicted feelings. As you read this, whatever your particular mood or feelings, hear our Master respond to your question, "What can I do for this aching inside?" With a smile and outstretched arms he responds, "Has no one condemned you? Neither do I! Do you love me? Then join in caring for others who have hurt and failed as you might have." In this is Christ's hope and peace.

Personal Reflection or Group Discussion

1. For an opening exercise, do a simple drawing of a person—a stick figure is fine. Ask the group to name all the ways we can recognize when someone is depressed. Write the terms they name on the part of the stick figure where these terms fit.

2. Think about the people you know, folks important in your life. Who among them are part of those 20 million Americans suffering from depression?

3. Recall the saddest time in your life. Did that time have clear identifiable causes, or did it just come? What were the factors that contributed to your sadness? What were the wisest things you did to deal with the sadness? As you look back, what else might you have done?

4. In what way do the passages from Job 6 and 17 and Psalm 69 illuminate or inform any depression you may have felt?

5. What are the most helpful resources in your community to help a person dealing with grief, loneliness, sadness, and depression? The most helpful resources in your church?

6. What does Jesus' question in John 8:11 have to offer a depressed person? How can that story interact with a person's depression?

7. What does the story in John 21:15-23 offer a sad or depressed person?

8. What other questions of Jesus and what other Bible passages would you add as resources for persons facing the issues this chapter mentions?

Chapter 6

Burnout and Fatigue

Our Question:

What can I do about my burnout and fatigue?

Jesus' Questions:

*Why do I speak to you at all? . . . . Why do you not understand
what I say?*
*You faithless and perverse generation, how much longer must I
be with you and bear with you?*
Do you believe I am able [and willing] *to do this?*

Scripture: Jn 8:12-58; Lk 9:37-43; Mt 9:27-38

Recently, I had lunch with a talented colleague. This is a person
who has brought great creativity and compassion to her difficult task
as a prison chaplain. The people she serves adore her, for she is present to their pain and offers a bit of warmth and light to a harsh environment. She is also able to bring both individuals and varied religious groups into closer fellowship and dialogue. Her work has been
acclaimed with awards from her denomination and seminary.

For all this, her on-site supervisors were not that supportive. Instead, there was bureaucratic bungling, institutional inertness, suspicion, resistance, and harassment. It was wearing on her. In spite of all
the good she was doing and all the people that needed her, this gifted
pastor was hanging on by her fingernails. She did not know how
much longer she could hang there.

Burnout? The question more experienced than asked. You see it in
the slumped shoulders of fatigue, hear it in the sigh of resignation,
and experience it in the lowered eyes of defeat and despair.

Burnout is a form of the depression we explored in Chapter 5, but it
is a very specific form, for it is connected to one's ideals and the effort

one has put forth to express those ideals. This question comes in a variety of forms from people of all ages. However asked, it boils down to this: What can I do about my burnout, tedium, and compassion fatigue?

A team of researchers did a study of burnout among hospital nurses who were working with terminally ill cancer patients. Those who volunteered for this nursing assignment were highly idealistic persons who wanted to help people and cared deeply about their patients. However, a number of factors caused this enthusiasm to wane. For one thing, the work was hard and discouraging; it was painful to draw close to people and then lose them. Furthermore, very sick patients and frightened families are not in a frame of mind to give considerate, grateful responses. Without realizing it, most of these nurses began to do things to protect themselves from being overwhelmed by the situation. Bit by bit, they emotionally detached themselves from their patients. Occasionally, they engaged in a kind of gallows humor. They discovered themselves resenting the very people whom they thought they wanted to help.

When these things happened, the guilt and shame they felt was enormous. They would think something like, "I, of all people, am not supposed to be feeling this way." Some of the nurses told that while "they felt miserable on the inside, they tried to look crisp, efficient, sometimes even ebullient on the outside." In turn, they would look around and think the other nurses were coping well, and so they might conclude, "Most people around here seem to be doing okay, therefore there must be something wrong with me. Perhaps I'm too delicate or hypersensitive; maybe I'm going crazy; I must not be cut out to be a nurse." They placed blame on themselves rather than seeing it as a response to a highly stress-producing situation, so powerful it affects practically everyone the same way.[1] They were in a downward spiral of burnout. (We will return to their story later.)

Although these nurses were in an extremely stressful situation, many others experience something very similar. Increasingly, educators feel it. I have heard teachers say, "I went into teaching because I loved helping people learn. More and more I contend with harsh discipline problems, unmotivated students, complaining parents, increasing paperwork, and at times fear for my own safety." Persons in many kindred occupations often feel a similar way.

People burn out on church as well. Numbers of church volunteers often feel exploited, taken for granted, overextended. A recent study[2] showed an increasing interest among Americans in spirituality, but not a corresponding interest in churches. Some feel that while they'd love help on their spiritual search, their experience is that churches ask more of them than they have time or energy to give. So they choose to do their search by themselves, or, increasingly, on the Internet. Indeed, some futurists, noting existing trends, predict that in ten years, from 10 to 20 percent of the population will rely exclusively on the Internet for their religious and spiritual needs.

These days, often people feel unable to respond to things that used to help. When I was a pastor, I would recruit persons for a lay ministry program that entailed fifty hours of training in a number of human relations and ministry skills. This was followed by two years of a commitment to caring listening and supervision. Frequently, people would respond to that invitation with such words as "I would love to do that. It sounds like such a growing-edge experience. I wish I had the time to devote to it."

Then later, after these lay ministers had been trained (those who could and did respond), I would offer someone the services of one of these lay ministers as a caring listener and friend. Hurting people would often respond, "It would be good to have such a caring friend, but I do not know how I'd work that person into my schedule!"

Burnout reveals itself in many ways. It shows up in *physical exhaustion*—low energy, chronic fatigue, weakness, and weariness, accident proneness, increased susceptibility to illness, headaches, nausea, muscle tension, and more. Burnout also shows up in *emotional exhaustion,*—feelings of depression, helplessness, hopelessness, and entrapment. One person put it this way,

> A few years ago, I felt that life was an eternal feeling of exuberance and joy. I liked my work and had a very active social life. Now I feel my job is a dead end. My emotional resources are drained; my best friends irritate me. I do not know my children and I do not have the emotional energy to be their friend. I find it hard to be polite and tolerant of my clients. I became immersed in self-pity and all I want is to be left alone.[3]

Burnout shows up in *mental exhaustion*—the development of negative attitudes toward one's self, work, and life. This leads one to feel inadequate, inferior, and incompetent. The manager of a public agency said,

My hands are tied and I feel useless and impotent. I never have
enough information for making a decision in my work. I cannot
deal effectively with the requirements of my job. I feel worthless
like a total failure and I resent my subordinates who witness this
failure.[4]

Burnout shows up in *spiritual exhaustion.* The joy, certainty, and
power one once felt in one's faith departs. Worship and prayer which
once revived and renewed, begins to feel like one more obligation.
There may be feelings of disappointment, of betrayal, of guilt. One
person commented, "I felt like my soul was dying."

Author Leonard Woolf once wrote, "I look back on my life and feel
I have accomplished practically nothing. After all those books and
committee meetings, the world isn't much different than if I had spent
all the time playing ping-pong. I have to conclude that I have wasted
150,000 to 200,000 hours!"[5] That is the voice of a burned-out person.

What contributes to burnout? Pastoral counselor Lloyd Rediger
has identified ten factors, all of which play a part. Here is Lloyd's list:

1. The gap between expectations and reality: Either my too-high
   expectations of myself, or others' too-high expectations of
   me.
2. Double binds: People feel trapped; no matter what they do
   they can't win. Sometimes to meet one need, a person has to
   ignore another.
3. High-intensity living: Falling into the temptation to consume
   more, try harder, and win at everything one does.
4. Something-to-prove agenda, a chip on one's shoulder, a feeling that one must prove oneself to others by succeeding at all
   costs.
5. Energy drainers: Some go through life with "monkeys on their
   backs," such as alcoholism, drug addiction, or time-wasting
   habits that drain energy.
6. Lack of affirmation from people whose opinions matter to me.
7. Role pressures: Sometimes it is not the work expectations, but
   the expectation of the kind of person one will be, what one's
   spouse will be, what one's family will be that wears one out.
8. The loner lifestyle: Unavailability or unwillingness to reach
   out to others for support and care.

9. Life formulas that will disappoint you: For example, "If I give my all to my work, my employer will certainly meet all my needs."
10. Attitudes: Life has its ups and downs. Some see problems as opportunity for growth. Others see the downs as unfair, unjust; evidence that "they're all against me."[6]

So far, I have given you a quick thumbnail sketch of what burnout is, how it manifests itself in a person, and some of the things that cause it. Did you recognize yourself in anything I have told you so far? If so, we are ready to hear some questions from Jesus.

What does Jesus say to those who may be exhausted or burned out? Jesus' first set of questions may surprise us. These questions occur on two levels of intensity. We hear the relatively mild intensity in the eighth chapter of John. John portrays Jesus as offering himself as light of the world to a people who are stubborn, unbelieving, and resisting. Each revealing statement he makes is met by cross-examination and criticism. In the midst of this discussion (really more an unfair debate), Jesus exclaims, *"Why do I speak to you at all?"* (Jn 8:25). Later in the same conversation, he asks, *"Why do you not understand what I say?"* (Jn 8:43). As John writes the drama of divine light contending with human darkness, he offers these examples of frustration and disappointment in the light bringer.

In the next question, the intensity has increased tremendously. *"You faithless and perverse generation, how much longer must I be with you and bear with you?"* (Lk 9:41). Jesus and those closest to him had just come from the experience we describe as the "Mount of Transfiguration." The gospel descriptions of that event are couched in mystery. His clothes became "dazzling white." His disciples saw him conversing with Moses and Elijah "about his departure." A voice from heaven had spoken, "This is my Son, My chosen; listen to him!" It had been a luminous moment. As beautiful as it was, the time came to return to the rest.

As they descend the mountain, they encounter a suffering child, a distraught father, embarrassed and inept disciples, and a crowd that was getting out of control. The desperate father begged Jesus for help. It was at this point that Jesus exploded, *"You faithless and perverse generation, how much longer must I be with you and bear with you?"* Some Bible scholars want to escape the scandal of this question. They point out that the verse is a reminiscence of Deuteronomy 32:5, and that it does accurately portray the world to which Jesus came. That all may be. However, at the same time no other verse so vividly portrays a loving, compassionate Jesus on the verge of burnout! There was deep, understandable, human frustration in that question. Would the pain never end? The suffering people ever quit coming? The complaints, ineptitude, conflicts ever cease? Was it worth it? After that glorious mountaintop, this mess before him seemed so convoluted, that, for one brief moment, he gave voice to his frustration. After that, Jesus "rebuked the unclean spirit, healed the boy, and gave him back to his father" (Lk 9:42b). In spite of his frustration, Jesus did what he was called to do for this child and father, "and all were astounded at the greatness of God" (Lk 9:43).

So what do these stories say to us about our burnout and fatigue? At least this, that the one from God who entered into human flesh was made like us in every respect—including the inclination to discouragement and frustration. This passage tells us that Jesus knows us and the experiences of frustration and burnout better than we might imagine. The Bible verses also tell us that Jesus, frustrated though he was, did what he needed to do. He brought help to needy persons even though the joy may not have been in it for him as it once was.

That is a start, but there is more to be found in the teachings and questions of Jesus. As we move to another question Jesus asked, a little story may prepare us. Two woodcutters worked the entire day at their labor. One worked all day long without stopping even for an occasional rest. The other woodcutter worked steadily, but would pause every so often for a break. At the end of the day, his pile was larger than his companion's though he had not worked as many minutes.

"How can this be possible?" asked the first woodcutter. "I never stopped working!" Responded the other, "It's simple—when I stopped to rest, I also sharpened my ax."[7]

What sharpens your ax and mine, so that we can keep at our many pressures and tasks without burning out? This brings us to our next scripture passage.

Two blind men—suffering from a widespread malady in Jesus' day, cry out publicly, in front of a crowd, "Have mercy on us, Son of David." Jesus did not respond until he entered a house. Then the needy persons came to him and talked with him privately there. Face to face, his first word to them was a question; *"Do you believe that I am able to do this?"* Ponder that for a moment. Two people said they wanted Jesus' help. We say we want Jesus' help—we are overwhelmed, swamped, fatigued, burned out. Jesus responds with a question, *"Do you believe that I am able to do this?"* If they answered yes, and were right, they would have to live with the consequences of that. There would be no more sympathy, no more begging, and no more being taken care of. But they would also live with the glorious adventure of sight!

The same question comes to us. If we answer "yes," then we are forced to ask if we are willing to accept this help. We are also led to explore what we can do to make life different, and what would we do if life were different.

This question leads us deeper, causing us to ask: Does our present state of confusion and exhaustion have the last word? Or, do we believe that we live in the strength of one who is greater than our weakness? Are we willing to trust the strength of the one that is able? Does that possibly mean letting go of something that we thought we alone could do?

Although, burnout is partly a psychological problem, it is more basically a spiritual and theological problem. Behind burnout lie such questions as: "Who is God? Is God able? Is God concerned and involved? What of my burden can I give to God and the caring persons God places around me?" All of this is in Jesus' question, *"Do you believe I am able to do this?"*

When we hear and answer those questions, we also discover the inner-life ways of "sharpening our ax." It might mean prayers such as "Lord, help me be wise in regard to decisions about my time and I will obey." "Lord, help me to work when I work, play when I play, rest when I rest, and pray when I pray." "Lord, help me to know that I do not labor alone, but that I labor with you and your mighty power dwelling in me."

Let us return to the study of nurses who were burning out. Do you know the first thing the researchers did to help them? It seemed so simple. They called a number of them together and asked each one to write on a piece of paper their five greatest points of stress in their work. Then they turned to one another in smaller groups and shared what they had written. The researchers reported an electric atmosphere in the room as they did this. Emotions of laughter and tears, relief, and great joy were expressed. Each felt alone in the struggle, withdrawn, discouraged, and angry. When they discovered their co-workers were all contending with similar emotions, there was relief beyond words. They could give support to one another. They were on their way back to being able to serve longer and well.

This squares with the experience of my chaplain friend. Over our lunch, I asked her, "In the face of all this resistance, what keeps you going?" She responded, "Times like this—with you and with my other friends."

All of this points to a means of renewal Christ has given each of us. Churches have been rediscovering the small-group movement. One of the purposes of these groups is to help people with the very issue we have been discussing. Persons can come together, relax, and become honest about the stress and pain in their lives. Group members offer support, listening, friendship, and prayer support. *"Do you believe I am able to do this?"* Then test out my power in one of my small groups.

The later verses (Mt 9:27-38) in our Scripture lesson give further perspective. These verses refine Jesus' question and offer an implied question; *"Do you believe I am able [and willing] to do this?"* This Scripture goes on, "Then Jesus went about all the cities and villages, teaching in their synagogues, and proclaiming the good news of the kingdom and curing every disease and every sickness. When he saw the crowds, he had compassion for them because they were *harassed* and *helpless,* like sheep without a shepherd" (italics added). Those two words are powerful in the Greek language and have many meanings. One translator says that the people Jesus saw were "bewildered and miserable." Another translates it, "for they were bewildered and dejected, like sheep without a shepherd."

Does Jesus' expressed compassion for those pressured, harassed crowds connect to our feelings of burnout and fatigue? Does his description of them ("like sheep without a shepherd") fit how you and I feel some days? Sheep are nearsighted, prone to wandering, easily frightened, likely to scatter. Does that fit? Sheep are also able to hear the shepherd's voice and follow. The shepherd speaks of his love and care for folks such as you and me.

Jesus goes on to use another term to describe those people (and us), "The harvest is plentiful, but the laborers are few. . ." (Mt 9:37). We are not only sheep without a shepherd, we are harvest. The very term "harvest" implies: we are closer to fruition than we had imagined; we are promise, the reason the farmer has labored so hard; we are crown and climax of all the farmer's effort. How does the "farmer" feel about the "harvest?" The farmer welcomes each part of the harvest with justifiable pride and great joy!

Within this implied question is another: "How do you feel about yourself and other people?" Jesus reminds us that he has compassion for us, when we are harassed, helpless, bewildered, miserable, dejected. He also suggests an explanation of why we may have these feelings. They happen when we live like sheep without the shepherd. Jesus sees himself as the one who waits to be shepherd of our souls. He also sees us as rich harvest, ripe for the reaping, not as others of his day saw us—as chaff to be scattered and burned.

We have been exploring our own burnout and fatigue. In response, we have heard a series of questions from Jesus. The first ones revealed his struggle with this very issue. First it was relatively mild, *"Why do I speak to you at all?" "Why do you not understand what I say?"* Then it was severe indeed, *"O faithless and perverse generation, how much longer must I be with you and bear with you?"* Our further exploration brought us before a powerful question from our Lord; *"Do you believe that I am able to do this?"* Then, a refinement of that question, *"Do you believe I am able [and willing] to do this?"* When you answer yes, there is wisdom and power to guide and strengthen.

How this will happen may not be clear. The way in which it will happen may not be sudden. The one who found sustained power again and again during his own life has the power to interact with the burnout in ours. Do you believe Jesus is able to do this?

Personal Reflection or Group

1. For an opening exercise, have participants do what the nurses mentioned in this chapter did—write down the five areas of greatest stress in their life. Ask them to consider, "What do you see? Are there any surprises?" Now have them share this list with one to three other persons and listen to their lists. Ask them, "What do you discover as you hear what one another is experiencing?"
2. Remember the time of greatest stress and burnout in your past. What contributed to your getting there? If you overcame it, what helped you find renewal?

3. Review "Lloyd's list" of factors that contribute to burnout. Which are you experiencing?

4. What was your response to the author's suggestion that Jesus struggled with this issue as well? Was it hard to accept? If accepted, does it offer anything to your journey?

5. Read Matthew 9:27-38 slowly and reflectively. What words stand out to you? With what persons in the Scripture do you identify? What good news do you hear?

6. What steps of self-care and spiritual renewal will you take to help you deal with your burnout?

Part II.
Probing the Divine Depth:
A Dialogue Between Our Questions
and Jesus' Questions About God's
Way with Us

Chapter 7

God's Love

Our Question:

How can I know God loves me?

Jesus' Questions:

> *Which of you having a hundred sheep . . . does not . . . go after the one that is lost . . . ?*
> *Which of them will you love . . . more?*
> *Is it not written, "My house shall be called a house of prayer for all the nations"?*
> *Who is greatest?*
> *What more could I do? (Implied)*

Scripture: Lk 15:3-10, 7:36-50, 22:24-30; Mk 11:15-19; Is 5:1-4

A group of women, most of them in their thirties and forties, eagerly gathered for their regularly scheduled [church group] session. They did so with enthusiasm for a wise and respected older woman had agreed to come and discuss a popular new novel that dealt with last things. The group came to order and the guest leader spoke. Soon they were involved in lively discussion. They left the novel behind and, in this free, accepting environment, talked about the deepest mysteries and longings of their lives. Then the discussion took another direction as they reflected, "Of all the questions we have raised, which is the most important, the most urgent with us?" Quite quickly they agreed that their most pressing question is, "How can I know God loves me?"

The guest leader, a pastoral counselor and marriage therapist was not surprised. It is a question she hears again and again in her counseling practice.

Is there such a thing as real love, divine love in an often-loveless world? Most of the persons in this women's support group asking this question had not undergone catastrophic illness or accident that challenged a once-cherished belief in God's love. Some were experiencing loss—of children going to school, of parents aging, of friends moving. For the most part, they lived from day to day in our kind of world, a world in which many love things and use people, and they wondered.

A few came from stable families where they had felt relatively secure in their parents' love, but several did not. Some recalled earlier loves in their lives, covenants to love another person forever. Some were struggling to hold things together and keep that promise, while others were part of that 50 percent of our married population where promises of eternal love have not been kept.

The pressure to get ahead with its corresponding time crunch, the relentless competition, the lean-and-mean employment market—all this and more can leave one bruised and wondering, "I don't readily see evidence that others love me. Why should I believe God does?" Their question is our question. In every pew there is at least one broken heart. We wonder as well.

The hymn "There's a Wideness in God's Mercy" promises that ". . . the heart of the eternal is most wonderfully kind." Is it true? Does God's love still exist in an often-loveless world? Does God love me as I am, warts and all? Does God's love cover me like a garment, course in my veins, reach down into that inner, secret part of me that I'd rather others do not see? How can I know God loves me?

The New Testament is filled with ringing declarations on this topic, as the folks in this group well knew. But still they asked. Perhaps a less direct method will provide some clues, some opportunities for discovery. It may be that in the questions of Jesus we will be led to discover and claim whatever truth there is for each of us on this topic. So let us turn to some questions Jesus asked us.

We start with two of Jesus' famous parables that are also questions, *"Which one of you, having a hundred sheep and losing one of them, does not leave the ninety-nine in the wilderness and go after the one that is lost until he finds it? When he has found it, he lays it on his shoulders and rejoices. . . Or what woman having ten silver coins, if she loses one of them, does not light a lamp, sweep the house, and search carefully until she finds it?* When she has found it, she calls together her friends and neighbors saying, 'Rejoice with me, for I have found the coin that was lost'" (Lk 15:4-9).

In addition, consider these questions Jesus asked as he was about to heal a hurting person on the Sabbath, "Does not each of you on the Sabbath untie his ox or his donkey from the manger, and lead it away to give it water? And ought not this woman, a daughter of Abraham whom Satan bound for eighteen long years, be set free from this bondage on the Sabbath day?" (Lk 13:15-16). Another verse, again on the appropriateness of healing on the Sabbath, "If one of you has a child or an ox that has fallen into a well, will you not immediately pull it out on a Sabbath day?" (Lk 14:5); and, a question we quoted in Chapter 3, "Is there any one among you who, if your child asks for a fish, will give a snake instead of a fish? Or if the child asks for an egg will give a scorpion?" (Lk 11:11-12).

Although there are differences and nuances in these questions, all of them have a common thread: look to the best in human care—your care of others and others' care of you. Think how you respond to the need, routine or urgent, of animals, and of your children. You do this out of love, or at least consideration. Our human love is a sign for us of God's love. Of course with God, there is always a "how much more" dimension.

Do a little experiment and shut your eyes for a moment. Now in your mind's eye, visualize the person or persons who thought you were extra special. Remember those folks whose eyes lit up when you came in the room, who thought everything you did was wonderful, who believed in you. Visualize a particular time you met those persons and recall the encounter.

I hope you were able to recall someone. For me the answer came quickly. I saw two persons, my mother and my hometown pastor. This (female) pastor and my mom became close friends and lived together in the closing years of their lives. In their latter, frail years, I would travel to see them from time to time, hoping to be of some help. Instead, *they* would ignore arthritic pain to prepare cinnamon rolls and chocolate chip cookies and home-cooked meals for me. They would receive my simple errands and chores with great appreciation and would praise and encourage my every effort. They were so proud of me. Far beyond my deserving, I was loved!

Now do another experiment. Visualize the person or persons to whom you give that unconditional love or acceptance. Perhaps a friend, a pal, a niece, a nephew, maybe a spouse, a lover, a child, or grandchild. As you visualize that person to whom you give unconditional love, no questions asked, recall one encounter with that person.

Let me tell you the person and picture that came to my mind. I provide just a little background. Shortly before my fiftieth birthday, our oldest daughter and son-in-law told us we would be grandparents. Turning fifty and becoming a grandpa sounded like aging to me, something I did not do gracefully. On the other hand, my wife Mary Ann, who is younger than I, was excited, buying and making things for the baby. I struggled with depression and resistance. However, as the time drew near, I found myself warming to the subject and telling a Bible study group of older women about the coming birth. Then the baby was born, and he was given my name as his second name. I told the women of his birth and one of them said to me, "Dick, now you are going to learn what love really is." A month later, when I finally got to see him, I was drawn to him like a magnet. Though allowing others their turns with him, awake or asleep, he and I were together. Daniel Richard is now twenty and has been joined by five other grandchildren. Similar experiences of unconditional love occurred every time a new grandchild was born. If you pushed me to identify one source of joy in my life, one reason for living and building a better world, I would point to those six children.

How can we know God loves us? We look to familiar places and people, the love we received, and the love we gave. Scripture tells us not only to love, but also to recognize God in the midst of that love. Though it is not proof, it is a sign of God's love among us.

We move on to another question of Jesus, another indicator: "A certain creditor had two debtors; one owed five hundred denarii, and the other fifty. When they could not pay, he canceled the debts for both of them. *Now which of them will love him the more?*" Jesus' question was offered in the middle of a dinner party given by Simon the Pharisee. Simon had treated him rather rudely and coldly without the customary courtesies. During the meal, a woman "who was a sinner" bathed his feet with her tears, wiped them with her hair, kissed his feet, and anointed them with ointment. Simon was offended, both at the woman's behavior and at Jesus' allowing it. It was at this point that Jesus asked his question. Simon answered correctly, and so would we—the person who knows one is forgiven of the greater debt will probably love the more. What does this tell us about knowing that God loves us? It invites us to look directly at what God has done for us so far. What debts have we had cancelled? What unconditional acceptance given? What opportunities, gifts, people that are far beyond our deserving have we received?

In her lively book, *Traveling Mercies,* Anne Lamott describes receiving such unexpected costly love. She was born into a family that did not believe in God. Even as a child, there was some impulse in her to believe and pray, but she did it secretly. She was drawn first to a Catholic family and then a Christian Science family—families of her friends. She envied their peace, faith, and regular worship practices. However, she and her family only attended occasional special holiday services in her childhood and youth.

Years later, life was not going well for her as an adult. She was struggling with a series of unsuccessful romances, an uncertain career, bulimia, drug overuse, and alcoholism.

On Sundays she went to a flea market, where, from the street, she heard the singing in a tiny African-American Presbyterian Church. She went to the door of the church to listen, but refused to sit down. She took off when the preaching began.

She returned from time to time. Eventually, after a few months, she would come a little further inside and sit in a folding chair off by herself. As she describes it:

> Then the singing enveloped me. It was furry and resonant, coming from everyone's very heart . . . the music was breath and food. Something inside me that was stiff and rotting would feel soft and tender. Somehow the singing wore down all the boundaries and distinctions that kept me so isolated. Sitting there, standing with them to sing, sometimes so shaky and sick that I felt like I might tip over, I felt bigger than myself, like I was being taken care of, tricked into coming back to life. But I had to leave before the sermon.[1]

As time went on and crises mounted, she began to sense the presence of Jesus near her, in her home, on the road, at church. Finally, she overcame all her prejudices about Christians and said to this presence "[Expletive] I quit." She continues, "I took a long deep breath and said out loud, 'All right, You can come in.' So this was my beautiful moment of conversion."[2]

This group of strangers became her family and mediated to her the very love and presence of Jesus. It began as I described it but has continued for some years since, with church people providing support in the birth of her son. Poor people slipped her money when her career was floundering. This church was her steadying force as she overcame alcoholism, drug addiction, and bulimia. Strangers, their songs, and their care brought her God and God's love when she least expected and greatly resisted such an experience.

We go on to another related question of Jesus: *"Is it not written, 'My house will be called a house of prayer for all the nations'?"* (Mk 11:17a). This question occurred in a moment of Jesus' great anger and decisive action. He looked at God's sacred temple and saw that one part of it had been made into an emporium or a bazaar. This part was the outer court, the "Court of the Gentiles," the only part of the temple where a devout pagan could come to pray, meditate, and seek the God of Israel. With all the hawking of wares and the noise, reek, and waste of animals, there was now no place for pious God seekers to come and pray. With outrage, Jesus drove out those merchants, shouting his question,—*Is this not a place for all the nations to pray?* Some people thought it didn't matter. To Jesus it mattered greatly!

So what does this tell us about God's love for us? Simply this, that the more clearly we see the vast breadth of God's love, the more clearly we see how it touches us. When we see that God loves some people entirely unlike us, those who are not attractive, those who have failed terribly, then we gain a further inkling of God's care for us.

George F. Regas recalls a conversation with Desmond Tutu, bishop in the Church of South Africa. Tutu said,

> George, you know I was raised in the Anglo-Catholic tradition of our church. We would have on the altar a tabernacle in which we would place the consecrated bread and wine—those elements made holy by God. And every time we would come by that tabernacle we would genuflect, we would bow our knee in respect for God's presence at the altar. You know, I feel, George, like genuflecting every time a white person or black person comes across my path. Bowing before them because they are vessels of the holy and living God.

George Regas reflected,

> I could hardly imagine that. In that cauldron of violence and bitterness and hatred, Archbishop Desmond Tutu sees in every

person the worth they have because they are the children of God. That's why his life shines as a light to the world.[3]

Near the end of *Traveling Mercies,* Anne Lamott tells of an ugly experience that led her to this same truth. She, her son, and their dog were on a tiny California beach when a man came to the beach with a big golden retriever on a leash. The two dogs touched noses and sniffed each other. The man tugged at the leash to lead his dog away. When the dog did not immediately come, the man picked up a thick stick and smashed into the dog's rib cage—once and again. The dog did not even yelp, but Sam, Anne's son did. Later the man showed further cruelty in yanking the dog around. Children and parents were at a loss how to stop this cruelty. Anne reflected that while Jesus would probably have been able to protect the dog and love the dog abuser at the same time, that was beyond her. Although Jesus might have seen the dog beater's fear and need, she finds herself "more into blame and revenge," as well as the comfort of self-righteousness. Some of them did run off to report this to nearby police. Still, she found herself feeling shamed at what she saw and her inability to be of any help to anyone. As she sought to make sense of it all, she reflects.

> The mystery of God's love as I understand it is that God loves the man who was being mean to his dog just as much as he loves babies; God loves Susan Smith who drowned her two sons as much as he loves Desmond Tutu. And he loved her just as much while she was releasing the handbrake of her car that sent her boys into the river as he did when she first nursed them. So of course he loves old ordinary me, even or especially at my most scared and petty and mean and obsessive. Loves me, *chooses* me.[4]

In accepting love from those who are strangers, of offering love, affirming love for those we find most difficult to accept, we make an experiential discovery. As did Anne Lamott, we learn something of God's love of us, as we are.

A pair of questions may guide us further on this quest. One part of this pair is implied; in actuality it comes from Isaiah in his song of the unfruitful vineyard, *"What more was there to do for my vineyard that I have not done in it?"* (Is 5:4). This quite readily yields a paraphrase, a question from God to us, God's people, *"What more could I do for you that I have not already done?"* This question can be put alongside Jesus' question, *"For who is greater, the one who is at the table or the one who serves? Is it not the one at the table? But I am among you as one who serves"* (Lk 22:27).

As we place these two questions together, the most basic and vivid understanding of God's love begins to emerge. What more could God do to communicate love? There was one more thing. In the vision of John's fourth Gospel, "And the word became flesh and lived among us, and we have seen his glory, the glory as of a father's only son, full of grace and truth" (Jn 1:14). Clarence Jordan, New Testament scholar and activist, once commented on this verse by noting that God must have concluded that we were deaf, but we could still see! The word became flesh, living among us, where we could see this gift, full of grace and truth.

The one who came reminded us by his question that he came as a servant, responding to pain and feeding the hungry—both physically and spiritually. He proclaimed a gentle kingdom of love, justice, and obedience and invited all, no matter what their background or sin, to come and enter in.

There was no end to the servant role Jesus readily accepted, "No one has greater love than this, to lay down one's life for one's friends" (Jn 15:13). Jesus did just that.

The medieval mystic Julian of Norwich spoke to her vision of Jesus on the cross and asked, "If I were the only one, would you have done that for me?" Jesus is said to have responded to her, "Over and over and over again, if necessary."[5]

The twelfth-century theologian Peter Abelard unforgettably proclaimed the cross as an expression of love above all else. He once expressed his powerful theology in a beautiful little hymn:

> Alone Thou goest forth O Lord
> In sacrifice to die;
> Is this Thy sorrow nought to us
> Who pass unheeding by?

> Our sins, not thine, Thou bearest, Lord,
> Make us Thy sorrow feel,
> Till through our pity and our shame
> Love answers Love's appeal.[6]

Love answers love's appeal! That's the ultimate testimony to love in a sometime loveless world. That's the final answer to the question, "How can I know God loves me?" As we have pondered this most basic question, Jesus' questions stimulate us to look at the deepest love we have ever given or ever received. We are invited to consider the great debts cancelled, the wonderful gifts given, and to love much because of it. We are compelled to look at the most unlikely persons that God loves and to allow that God loves us as well. Then we are led to look long and deeply at the cross until "love answers love's appeal."

Perhaps out of these experiences, we are ready to say with Benjamin Disraeli, "We are all born for love; it is the only principle of existence and its only end."[7] Perhaps, also, we are ready to claim as our own those ringing New Testament declarations about God's love. "But God proves his love for us in what while we still were sinners, Christ died for us" (Rom 5:8). "In this is love, not that we loved God but that [God] loved us and sent [the] son to be the atoning sacrifice for our sin" (1 Jn 4:10). As biblical theologian C. E. B. Cranfield notes, "All that the New Testament has to say about the love of God . . . is expressed in two words, 'Jesus Christ.'"[8]

Personal Reflection or Group Discussion

1. For an opening exercise, invite people to do what was suggested in the early pages of this chapter: remember one person and one incident in which they received unconditional love; and one person and one incident in which they gave unconditional love. Invite them to turn to one other person and hear each other's stories.
2. What makes it most difficult for you to believe God loves you?
3. What makes it possible for you to believe God loves you?
4. The chapter contains some examples of individuals or groups making real God's love to another. What stories do you have to tell of similar deeds or occasions?
5. What Bible questions would you add to those in this chapter?
6. What other Bible passages or teachings help you answer the question of this chapter?

Chapter 8

Prayer

Our Question:

What is prayer?

What happens when I pray?

How can I pray more effectively?

Jesus' Questions:

Why do you put . . . primary things second?
Who touched me?
Where are the nine?
Why are you afraid?
Could you not watch with me one hour?

Scripture: Mt 6:5-8, 8:26, 26:36-46; Mk 5:31; Lk 17:17-19

We live in two worlds when it comes to prayer.

On the one hand, we live in a world that sees prayer as absolutely foundational, basic, and essential for a firsthand religious faith. Consider these quotes from leading Christians of recent times:

> Elton Trueblood: "Prayer is the heart of genuine religion."[1]
> Thomas Keating: "Prayer and meditation are divine psychotherapy."[2]
> John Casteel: "Prayer is a term for dialogue between God and us."[3]
> Barry and Ann Ulinov: "The only way we know anything about God is through praying."[4]
> Richard Foster: Prayer is ". . . a love relationship, an enduring, continuing, growing love relationship with the great God of the Universe." Prayer is "finding the heart's true home."[5]

Olive Wyon: "As the body lives by breathing, so the soul lives by praying."

Adolph Deissmann: "Wherever religion is vital in any human being, it is expressed as prayer."

Auguste Sabatier: "Where there is no prayer from the heart, there is no religion."

Samuel Coleridge: "The act of praying is the very highest energy of which the human heart is capable, praying, that is, with the concentration of the faculties."[6]

We could go on, but those witnesses are enough to remind us that which our hearts know and our Scriptures testify—namely that prayer is essential, foundational, and vital to a life of faith and discipleship. That's one world of prayer.

The other world is that of our own experience. In that world, we recognize that something is missing. We ask questions that run something like this: "What should I do when my prayers seem to hit the ceiling and come back to me? What about those times when it seems my prayers are only conversations with myself? Why does my mind wander so much when I try to pray, and what can I do about my short attention span and straying thoughts? If I pray, what difference is it supposed to make? When I pray and don't feel anything in particular, is my prayer still being heard? What happens when I pray? Are there more effective ways to pray?"

Our questions about prayer fall into two categories: one is the problem of unanswered prayer; the other is about learning this strange new/old language and practice of prayer. We will tackle the issue of answered and unanswered prayer in Chapter 9. In this chapter, we will live with our confusion, struggle, and uncertainty about prayer itself.

With our questions about prayer, we come to a wonderful source when we look at Jesus in the Gospels. In these brief, cryptic looks at Jesus' short career, there are at least fourteen different references to Jesus' own prayer life, his spoken prayers, or his teachings on prayer.

Jesus and his disciples lived in a religious heritage steeped in prayer, there were prayers for beginning and ending each day. With all that heritage of ritual prayers, the disciples seem to say to Jesus, "We have prayed all our lives, now teach us to pray." They had some of the problems with prayer we do. These disciples sensed that Jesus had grasped a deeper reality, had a more vital contact with almighty

God, found more in prayer, did more in prayer, discovered more in prayer, and received more in prayer than they did. Lifelong "prayers" that they were, they still humbly and urgently requested, "Lord, teach us to pray." One scholar notes, "Jesus prayed as naturally as a child breathes."[7]

Jesus taught a few things about prayer, and occasionally prayed aloud. He also responded to these questions by asking us questions about our prayer efforts. We will explore those questions, implied and direct. Jesus seems to be telling us, "Deep within, you have more wisdom about prayer than you are yet claiming. Hear my questions, and let them guide you to that untapped wisdom within."

In response to our questions about prayer, Jesus asks at least five questions in return. Jesus' first question of us is implied. It is this: *"Why do you put primary things second?"* This comes from Mt 6. Jesus first tells us what is secondary to avoid. "When you are praying, do not heap up empty phrases . . .[nor] think that [you] will be heard because of [your] many words. Do not be like [that] for your Father knows what you need before you ask."

That's secondary—many words, empty phrases, heaped up. This is guidance our age particularly needs. As Richard Rohr notes, a peril of our modern culture is "a glut of words, a glut of experiences, and yes, a glut of tapes, books, and ideas."[8]

Have you ever been around a person who talks nonstop, who seems to be able to talk even while inhaling air, who never stops for even a breath so *you* can jump into the conversation? If so, do you remember what happened? If you are anything like me, in spite of the many words—more probably because of them—you quit hearing *any* of the words!

In a similar way, something gets lost between God and us in the use of many words.

If the use of many words is secondary—what is primary? *Listening.* Listening in silence. Not being overly concerned whether any explicit or specific message comes or not. Just being there. Being still until we know God is God. Henri Nouwen writes, "Without solitude, it is virtually impossible to live a spiritual life."[9]

We have heard time and again about the importance of listening to another human being. In particular, counselors learn about how redemptive it is to be heard, *really* heard by another. Jesus' words take this a step further. He tells us that if we really listen to God, then we will be even more open, caring, and vulnerable to one another.

Anyone who has tried to listen to another knows how attention wanders from topic to topic. We should not be surprised if this happens in our own minds when we try to listen and be aware of the presence of God. We are called to be as patient with ourselves as we would be with a playful, wandering child, which is what we are. Listening is hard work!

In Mt 6, Jesus also speaks of another secondary matter: "And whenever you pray, do not . . . stand and pray in the synagogues and at the street corners, so that [you] may be seen by others." Surely Jesus is not condemning public prayer. However, for those of us who pray publicly—if we pray more publicly than privately, or if we pray more freely publicly than privately, we have a serious problem. We have put secondary things first, and there will be erosion of the power of prayer in our lives.

Jesus also makes quite clear what is primary: "But whenever you pray, go into your room and shut the door and pray to your Father who is in secret." What is primary? Presence, openness to friendship, comfort in the presence of God. It has been suggested "Prayer is the time exposure of the soul to God." You don't do time exposures in a hurry. Time, openness, friendship, without urgent pulse taking on how you are doing, that is what Jesus is urging. Patience with self and with God, allowing one's wandering mind to go and return, centering down behind closed doors in secret—that is what is primary. Richard Rohr points out,

> Prayer is not primarily saying words or thinking thoughts. It is, rather, a stance. It's a way of living *in* the Presence, living in *awareness* of the Presence, and even of enjoying the Presence. The full contemplative is not just aware of the Presence, but trusts, allows, and delights in it.[10]

With those powerful lessons, we are ready to hear yet more questions about how we pray.

Jesus' second question is this: *"Who touched me?"* (Mk 5:31).

Perhaps you remember the story. Jesus is rushing to the bedside of a young girl who is grievously ill, probably dying. As he rushes along, a suffering woman who has been afflicted with a constant menstrual flow of blood for twelve years desperately reaches out and touches the fringe of his robe. Immediately, she senses a healing charge, and he is aware that powerful virtue has gone out of him. So he turns and asks, *"Who touched me?"* When the woman confesses, Jesus gently concludes, "Daughter, your faith has made you well; go in peace, and be healed of your disease" (Mk 5:34).

With all the rush and pressure, why do you suppose Jesus stopped and asked this question? The woman would have been cured from the hemorrhaging either way. I believe that Jesus stopped because he wanted more for her. For prayer is more than magical reaching out for a secret gift (much as we would settle for that, all too often). Prayer is a relationship of trust and love, of openness and honesty. If only for a few minutes, Jesus and the woman met face to face, met in the deep places of their lives. She fell down and told him "the whole truth." In so doing, she experienced much more than a cure, wonderful as that was. This woman learned to be open and direct even with a powerful person, a divine person. She also felt Jesus' loving care, calling her daughter, empowering her, praising her faith, and encouraging her to live her new disease-free life.

Place that question beside this little parable:

> A famous Japanese sculptor once confounded the curators of an American art gallery where his works were being shown. At the base of each statue the sculptor had placed a polite little sign. The signs all read, PLEASE TOUCH.

Who touched me? Please touch.

A harassed laborer and lay preacher, tired of being teased, tested, and tormented by his co-workers. They loved to pull pranks on him to see if they could make the preacher cuss. He expressed his frustration one evening in a prayer, crying out about his weakness, his need of Christ's powerful touch. Gradually his prayer began to take the form of a song,

> I am weak but thou art strong. Jesus keep me from all wrong.
> I'll be satisfied as long as I walk, let me walk close to thee.
> Just a closer walk with thee, grant it Jesus is my plea.
> Daily, walking close to thee, let it be, dear Lord, let it be.[11]

He reached out for a touch and graced others with what he received.

A young pastor, Martin Luther King Jr., already the subject of bombing attacks and death threats, sat alone in his kitchen, feeling defeat and despair in his bones. He cried out for divine aid and discovered he was filled with a peace and that never again left him. As John Greenleaf Whittier's hymn, "Our Master" puts it, "We touch him in life's throng and press, And we are whole again."[12]

Who touched me? Please touch.

This brings us to Jesus' third question, which is, *"Where are the nine?"* (Lk 17:17).

Ten desperate lepers had cried out to him from the appropriate distance that lepers had to maintain. They shouted to him their appeal for mercy and healing. He responded to their pain and loneliness and told them to follow the custom and law, which was to go show themselves to the priests. In other words, he told them to begin to act as if they were healed. Along the way, they were indeed healed of that which had enslaved and isolated them. One, a Samaritan, when he saw he was healed, "turned back, praising God with a loud voice. He prostrated himself at Jesus' feet and thanked him" (Lk 17:15-16).

This led Jesus to ask, "Were not ten made clean? But the other nine, where are they? Was none of them found to return and give praise to God except this foreigner?" He added a word to the prostrate man before him, "Get up and go on your way; your faith has made you well."

The last phrase can also be translated "Your faith has saved you." There was indeed a deeper healing in not only being cured, but in acknowledging the love and grace of the one who provided the cure! Something was missing in the nine (and, quite possibly, in us) who have been richly blessed but fail in the common courtesy of acknowledged gratitude. Indeed, it is spiritually hazardous to be richly blessed and not recognize or acknowledge the source of that blessing.

Thanksgiving is the doorway to all prayer and right relationship with God and with others. If, after the listening and sense of presence, we don't know what to say in prayer, say thank you and expand on that gratitude endlessly.

Jesus' fourth question of us is this, *"Why are you afraid?"* (Mt 8:26).

The setting for this question was a trip across the Sea of Galilee when a sudden fierce squall came up. "A windstorm arose . . . the boat was being swamped by the waves . . . he was asleep." They awoke him with the cry, "Lord, save us, we are perishing!"

He did wake up from his much-needed sleep and asked them *"Why are you afraid, you of little of faith?"*

The answer is obvious: We are afraid Lord, because we tremble before thunder, lightning, hurricanes, tornadoes, earthquakes, El Niño, dictators, terrorists—we are afraid the earth is doomed. We are afraid of dying.

He has a question behind his question: "Don't you know that in prayer you are in the presence of one greater than your fears?" He rebuked the wind and the waves, and there was a great calm. His disciples who thought they knew him, found themselves asking a question of their own, "What sort of man is this, that even the winds and the sea obey him?" We have fears aplenty, but we are in the presence of one greater than our fears, one to whom we can turn.

Years ago, I had a humbling experience that I have always treasured. It was when our first child, Julie, was still a baby, probably a year old or so. A fierce lightning and thunderstorm came up one night. It woke her up, and she cried out with fright. I picked her up and handed her to her mother, as I shut the rest of the windows in the house. Mary Ann was comforting her, but somehow she sensed Mary Ann's unease and was still crying. When I returned, I lay down and put her on my chest. I don't know why, but I am not frightened of such storms. Immediately, she felt my calm and stopped crying in less than a minute. Within two minutes, she was sound asleep on my chest. I lay there, content and amazed at that interaction between us. When the storm ended, I put her back in her bed. When I am afraid, I hope to learn in a similar way to lean on the one who is calm and powerful and can be trusted. Why are you afraid? Will you surrender those fears to the one greater than our fears? This brings us to Jesus' fifth question: *"Could you not watch with me one hour?"*

This question comes from the last night of Jesus' life. They arrive at a place of temporary privacy, an olive grove and garden. Jesus, weighed down with all he must face, tells his closest friends, "I am deeply grieved even to death; remain here, and stay awake with me." With bloodlike sweat falling to the ground, he prayed that "this cup might pass" from him. Richard Foster writes,

> Jesus knew the burden of unanswered prayer. He really did want the cup to pass, and he asked that it would pass. "If you are willing" was his questioning, his wondering. The Father's will was not yet absolutely clear to him. "Is there any other way?" "Can people be redeemed by some other means?" The answer—no.[13]

This struggle makes us aware that the two worlds of prayer are not so far apart. Those mightiest in prayer—even Jesus—struggled with the same uncertainties, mixed motives, and uncertain answers as we do.

He prayed on and on until he was able to say, "If this cannot pass unless I drink it, your will be done" (Mt 26:42). Jesus had earlier taught us to pray, "Thy kingdom come, thy will be done. . ." It has been said that all prayer is summed up in those four words: "Your will be done." Jesus agonized in prayer through that lonely night until he was able to pray that prayer, even though it would cost him pain, torture, agony, and death itself.

However, he had to do it alone. His disciples, either too exhausted by the week before, or too paralyzed by the present, or too fearful of the future did not do one of the few things he ever asked of them. They did not watch with him, did not share his agony, did not enter into his wrenching struggle.

He prayed alone. Again and again he came to them and asked them to add their human comfort and support to the divine presence. He wanted words of love and encouragement. He wanted a small group to pray with him. But it did not happen. With lonely sadness he asked, "So, could you not stay awake with me one hour?"

Still our loving, suffering Savior agonizes over the world—its struggles, its hatreds, its self-destruction, and still he asks, "Will you watch with me, at least one hour?" For prayer is not only seeking God's presence in our lives personally, it is identifying with God's love for a suffering world. Prayer is responding to a Savior, who, amazingly, strongly wants our companionship.

We ask, "What happens when I pray, and how do I pray?" Our Lord's practices, teachings, and questions point to the certainty of an unseen world, caring and powerful beyond anything we have imagined. He asks, *"Why do you put second things first and first things second? Who touched me? Where are the nine? Why are you afraid?"* and, *"Could you not stay awake with me one hour?"*

Personal Reflection or Group Discussion

1. For an opening exercise, invite people to finish these phrases in as many ways as they can, "Prayer is. . . . According to Jesus, prayer is. . . ."

2. Do you have a favorite definition of prayer either from those provided in the chapter or elsewhere? If so, what is that definition? What important truths about prayer does it communicate?
3. Recall your most difficult time of praying, when you could not pray at all, or would pray only with great difficulty. What circumstances surrounded that experience of prayer?
4. Recall your richest time of prayer, not so much for answers as for a sense of presence and communion with God. What circumstances surrounded that experience of prayer?
5. Which of Jesus' questions cited in this chapter holds promise in your search to deepen your prayer life? In what ways?
6. What other questions of Jesus illuminate the heights and depths of prayer for you? What other Bible passages?

Chapter 9

Unanswered Prayer

Our Question:

Why is my prayer unanswered?

Jesus' Questions:

Do you want to be made well?
What is the first commandment?
Do you not know God is a loving parent?
Have I not promised to be with you to the ends of the earth?

Scripture: Jn 5:1-18; Mk 12:28-31; Lk 11:11-13; Mt 28:20

In *Huckleberry Finn,* Huck reflects on prayer. This is what he says:

> Miss Watson she took me in the closet and prayed, but nothing
> come of it. She told me to pray every day, and whatever I asked
> for I would get it. But it warn't so. I tried it. Once I got a fishline,
> but no hooks. It warn't any good to me without hooks. I tried for
> the hooks three or four times, but somehow I couldn't make it
> work. By and by, one day, I asked Miss Watson to try for me, but
> she said I was a fool. She never told me why, and I couldn't
> make it out no way. I set down one time back in the woods, and
> had a long think about it. I says to myself, if a body can get any-
> thing they pray for, why don't Deacon Winn get back the money
> he lost on pork? Why can't the widow get back her silver snuff-
> box that was stole? Why can't Miss Watson fat up? No, says I to
> myself, there ain't nothing in it.[1]

Huck overstates it, but he makes a point. Certainly, prayer is much
more than asking. Still, what are we to make of unanswered prayer?

Helmut Thielicke, a great German pastor and theologian once wrote,

> How often have we earnestly pled for something and haven't gotten it? All along the highway of our lives are there not the countless gravemarkers of unanswered prayers? Have we not all known bitter disappointment and moments when no voice nor answer came as we ardently prayed, and when we remained alone and disappointed in the silence?[2]

A faithful church member once handed me this note,

> Sometime would you preach a sermon on unanswered prayer. When you pray day after day, year after year for:
> - a friend with cancer and she dies;
> - kids with family problems and they get divorced;
> - estranged family members and they don't make up; and
> - for a health problem and even the doctors cannot cure it.
>
> Be sure to let me know when you talk about this. I want to hear it.

My friend gave voice to a cry of us all.

Such disappointments are exacerbated by the glowing testimonies of those who have had prayers powerfully answered. Not only are many persons convinced their prayers have been answered, such answers are increasingly being researched scientifically. Dr. Larry Dossey, is one who is giving much attention to the power of prayer in healing. In a recent article, "Prayer is Good Medicine," he tells of a former patient, a man dying from metastatic lung cancer. Round-the-clock prayers of his church upheld the man. Dr. Dossey sent him home to die, only to see the man recover and live for some years after that.

Dr. Dossey calls this healing by the prayers of others "nonlocal healing" or "distant healing" and points out that approximately 150 experiments have been performed in laboratories, clinics, and hospitals that tested the effect of prayer—or "distant healing." He reports that more than half of these studies have produced statistically significant results of healing or improvements. These experiments were with many types of illnesses.[3] Still the mystery remains. Why is some prayer answered with the response we desire and some not? Why did half of the prayer experiments produce scientifically significant results and the other half failed to do so?

We are on a topic that is important and visceral; another area in which all of the information, wisdom, and perspective are not yet in. I also struggle with this. For not only have I known the joy of prayer I saw as answered, but I have lived with disappointment. One of my favorite hymns has the line, "Teach me the patience of unanswered prayer." That needs to be the prayer of all of us.

As far as I can tell, Jesus never directly answered this question. Clearly he lived in an atmosphere of prayer, believed mightily in prayer, taught about the power of prayer, and practiced what he taught. At the same time, he asks us some questions. These questions respond to, and correspond with our questions. Let's consider four of them.

Question one from Jesus to us is this: *"Do you want to be made well?"* (Jn 5:6). On a Sabbath in Jerusalem, Jesus approaches a sick man beside the pool in Bethzatha. It was believed that an angel troubled the waters of the pool and the first one in after that would be healed. This man had been there for thirty-eight years and had somehow never been the first placed in the pool and healed. So Jesus asked him, *"Do you want to be made well?"*

The man avoids a direct answer. He says, I have no one to help me, others are ahead of me. He doesn't say, I want healing, health, and wholeness. When Jesus cures him of his lameness the man shows that he has problems aplenty still. He refuses to take responsibility for his action of carrying his stretcher on the Sabbath. When Jesus reveals himself to be his healer, this man immediately points Jesus out as the offender. One Bible commentator points out that by any usual standard, this man just wasn't worth Jesus' trouble. Although Jesus helped him with a lame body, this pitiful man chose to retain a lame spirit.

Still, Jesus asks each of us, do we really want the wholeness—all of the wholeness—for which we ask? Are we willing to invest ourselves thoroughly in the healing? Will we be the responsible, active, caring children of God that go with the answer yes?

Jesus' second question to us is one that was once put to him, *"Which is the first commandment?"* (Mk 12:28). In Lk 10:26, he responds to the question about what one must do to inherit eternal life with the question, "What is written in the law? What do you read there?" This question elicits the same response from another. We answer as he did, the first commandment is "You shall love the Lord your God with all your heart, and with all your soul, and with all your mind, and with all your strength. The second is this, You shall love your neighbor as yourself " (Mk 12:29-31).

A further question is asked, then. "Ponder that great commandment. In the light of it, do you understand why sometimes your prayers are not answered? Is it possible that the reason lies with you?" For our prayers to have a vital connection, they must come from a person who—as far as possible—has a clean conscience on the matters in these commandments.

Take the commandment to love thy neighbor. Charles Stanley writes, "I cannot go home on Sunday and yell at my wife for burning the chicken and then expect God to hear me when I ask [God] to bless the meal. That is hypocrisy." He adds, "Unresolved horizontal conflicts make for unresolved vertical conflicts."[4]

Or consider the commandment to love God with all our mind. That leads us to do some serious thinking about prayer. George Buttrick tells of the schoolgirl who was told that God could do anything. She had accidentally torn a page in her geography textbook. So she prayed that God would restore the page—and was greatly disappointed when the page remained the same.

We need to use our minds when we pray. In his classic book *Prayer,* Buttrick has a chapter titled "The Bounds and Boundlessness of Prayer." He confesses that we cannot finally know what are the bounds on prayer, and what is its boundlessness, but we cannot escape considering it. For example, we do not pray to undo an event that has already happened.

He readily recognizes that these bounds are hard to discern. He writes,

> But where the limits run who can closely trace? The land is vast and its bounds elude us. If a friend lost his hand in an accident we would not pray for a new hand to grow, but if he were sick with typhoid fever we would pray for his recovery. Where *is* the boundary? We would not pray for the sun to rise in the west, but if we were caught in the track of a forest fire we might pray for the wind to change. We would not pray for a youth to return to babyhood for a new start, but we would pray for good motives to kindle in him in power. Where *do* the limits run?[5]

These words were written some years ago. With the massive strides in medicine—including the recent transplant of a *hand,* does that expand—or, for that matter reduce—those things for which we pray? We don't exactly know how to answer these questions, but we must ask and then pray. Sometimes we pray wisely, sometimes not. Still, we continue with the faith that it is better to pray unwisely, perhaps naively, than not at all.

Consider the command to love God with all our strength. Pioneering missionary/Baptist minister William Carey urged, "Pray as if everything depends on God. Work as if everything depends on you." Prayer should never be a substitute for our own action. My home pastor used to say it was immoral to ask God to do something you can do yourself. It is also lazy to ask God to do what we can do ourselves. The wonderful old hymn states, "Christian rise and act your creed, let your prayer be in your *deed*." After we have done everything we can about any given problem—that is where our prayers of petition and intercession are to begin.

Jesus asks us: Have you prayed in obedience to the great commandment? That is a searching, hard question for us to live with. However, our leader's next question is much more gentle and reassuring. "Is there anyone among you who, if your child asks for a fish will give a snake instead of a fish? Or if the child asks for an egg will give a scorpion? If you [parents] . . . know how to give good gifts to your children, how much more will the heavenly [parent] give the Holy Spirit, [in another Gospel, the words are 'give good things'] to those who ask?" (Lk 11:11-13). In other words, whatever the apparent outcome of our prayers, *do we not know God is a loving parent* who wills for us the very best?

Sometimes we have requests that are deeply important to us. We feel we have done all we can, and we have prayed from a refined conscience. Still we do not receive. These are puzzling and hurtful to us. Yet even at such a time, we are called to claim these promises of God's care and love. Lloyd Ogilvie has noted, "There is a great difference between unanswered prayer and ungranted petitions."[6] In fact, many contend that all prayers are answered. Sometimes God says "yes," and sometimes God says "no," and sometimes God says "wait." As a matter of fact, sometimes God may be responding to a request even when it appears the answer is "no" or "wait."

In one of the most impressive passages in his "Confessions," St. Augustine pictures his mother, Monica, praying all one night, in a seaside chapel on the North African coast, that God would not let her son sail for Italy. She wanted Augustine to be a Christian. She could not endure losing him from her influence. If under her care, he still was far from being Christ's, what would be he in Italy, home of licentiousness and splendor, of manifold and alluring temptations? And even while she prayed there passionately for her son's retention at home, he sailed, by the grace of God, for Italy, where, persuaded by Ambrose, he became a Christian in the very place from which his mother's prayers would have kept him. The form of her petition was denied; the substance of her desire was granted. As St. Augustine himself puts it: "Thou, in the depth of thy counsels, hearing the main point of her desire, regardest not what she *then asked,* that thou mightest make me what she *ever desired*."[7]

The well-loved poem "He Prayed" by an unknown author leads us deeper into this same area as it speaks of God's responding to the cries of our hearts in different ways than we might have planned.

He prayed for strength that he might achieve;
He was made weak that he might obey.
He prayed for health that he might do great things;
He was given infirmity that he might do better things.
He prayed for riches that he might be happy;
He was given poverty that he might be wise.
He prayed for power that he might have the praise of men;
He was given weakness that he might feel the need of God.
He prayed for all things that he might enjoy life;
He was given life that he might enjoy all things.
He had received nothing that he asked for—all that he hoped for;
His prayer was answered—he was most blessed.[8]

Trust in *this* truth sustained Jesus through the most agonizing night of his life. As we ponder unanswered prayer, we return to a Gospel incident that we considered in Chapter 8. We come to Gethsemene, on the night before Jesus was to be killed. The Gospel of Mark tells us, Jesus "began to be distressed and agitated. And he said to them, 'I am deeply grieved, even unto death' . . .'" (Mk 14:33-34). Luke adds the detail, "In his anguish, he prayed more earnestly, and his sweat became like great drops of blood falling on the ground" (Lk 23:44). In this deep agony as he shared our full humanity, he prayed what any of us would have prayed, "Abba, Father, for you all things are possible; remove this cup from me. . ." That was the cry of his heart, and that part of the prayer was unanswered. Still trusting in "Abba"—loving parent God—Jesus went on to pray, "yet, not what I want, but what you want" (Mk 14:36). Trusting, Jesus endured the cross, rather than demanding acquiescence to his first prayer. He prayed believing what he had earlier taught, that God is like a loving parent, even when any evidence of that truth is hard to find.

This leads us to Jesus' fourth question; it is an implied question from our crucified and risen Lord: *"Have I not promised to be with you to the ends of the earth?"*

Of course, this chapter has not neatly answered all our questions about unanswered prayer. Even with the self-examining and awareness I have encouraged, still there are some unresolved questions, and some hard mysteries here. At times, when according to all *our* best understanding, it would have been better to have prayers answered in a different way.

Still, Jesus promises us that (as George Buttrick once put it) "no true prayer ever comes weeping home." When the answer we desire is not possible, still God may change the circumstances, or God may provide the person sufficient strength and power to endure and overcome.

I was deeply touched by a statement from the first missionary to Burma, Adoniram Judson, and by Harry Emerson Fosdick's comment on it.

Adoniram Judson, for example, made this statement at the close of his life: "I never prayed sincerely and earnestly for anything, but it came; at some time—no matter at how distant a day— somehow, in some shape—probably the last I should have devised—it came." But Judson had prayed for entrance into India and had been compelled to go to Burmah; he had prayed for his wife's life, and had buried both her and his two children; he had prayed for release from the King of Ava's prison and had lain there months, chained and miserable. Scores of Judson's petitions had gone without an affirmative answer. But *Judson* always had been answered. He had been upheld, guided, reinforced; unforeseen doors had opened through the very trials he sought to avoid; and the deep desires of his life were being accomplished not in his way but beyond his way.[9]

Still we ponder why some devout, heartfelt, selfless prayers are not answered in a way that seems fitting to us. Doubtlessly, we will wonder to the end of our days.

However, Jesus stands beside us and comforts us in this as he asks us, "Do you want to be made well?" "Do you reflect the two great commandments when you pray?" "Don't you know that God is a loving parent who wills for you the very best?" "Have I not promised to be with you to the ends of the earth?"

Personal Reflection or Group Discussion

1. For an opening exercise, have people join together in pairs. Then invite all to share with partners on two topics: (1) my most vivid experience of answered prayer; (2) my most puzzling experience of unanswered prayer.
2. What have been your most vivid experiences of answered prayer?
3. What have been your most frustrating experiences of unanswered prayer?
4. What teachings of Jesus—including but not limited to his questions—inform you as you ponder why prayers are not answered?
5. Comment on each of the questions Jesus asks of us in regard to prayer. How do each of these inform the mystery? Which make the mystery deeper? In what way?
6. Do you have questions about prayer beyond those we have discussed in Chapter 8 and Chapter 9 thus far? If so, what are your questions?
7. From your experience, what is the impact on the person who practices a life of systematic prayer?

Chapter 10

Suffering

Our Questions:

Why suffering?
Why do others suffer? Why do I?

Jesus' Questions:

Do you think that those who suffered were worse sinners?
Am I not to drink the cup that the father has given me?
My God, My God, why have you forsaken me?
Was it not necessary that the Messiah should suffer these things and then enter into his glory?

Scripture: Lk 13:2-4, 24:26; Jn 9:2-3, 18:11; Mt 27:56

Rowan Williams (now Archbishop of Canterbury) the Anglican bishop of Wales, was at Trinity Church on Wall Street on 9/11, a couple blocks from the World Trade Center when the planes crashed into the Twin Towers. He had traveled to New York City to record several hours of discussion regarding the issue of spirituality. That activity was immediately suspended so church leaders and members could be of compassionate help to all the traumatized, frightened, and confused people that came their way in the wake of that tragedy. Bishop Williams recalls,

> The morning after, very early, I was stopped in the street by a youngish man who turned out to be an airline pilot and a Catholic. He wanted to know what the hell God was doing when the planes hit the towers. What do you say? The usual fumbling about how God doesn't intervene, which sounds like a lame apology for some kind of "policy" on God's part, a policy exposed as heartless in the face of such suffering? Something

about how God is there in the sacrificial work of the rescuers, in the risks they take? I tried saying bits of this, but there was no clearer answer than there ever is. Any really outrageous human action tests to the limit our careful theological principles about God's refusal to interfere with created freedom. . . [This pilot] was a lifelong Christian believer, but for the first time it came home to him that he might be committed to a God who could seem useless in a crisis.[1]

This was a horribly vast experience of the mystery of undeserved suffering, one that caused a nation, indeed a world, to pause and wonder, to raise questions without answers.

At the same time, though, it was larger in scope, it was kindred to experiences that, in life and ministry, we see again and again.

- A "clean-living" woman, who never used tobacco products, struck down with lung cancer at age forty-nine.
- The loss of one partner from one of those beautiful marriages that ought to go on for years and years.
- An innocent child killed randomly in a drive-by shooting, another run over by his father who could not see him running out for a good-bye kiss.
- A third-world mother suffering childbirth complications that would be readily corrected in more developed countries.
- The far-too-premature death of someone upon whom many depended, a person needed for more years than the person lived.
- Tragic accidents with autos, farm equipment, or firearms involving people doing their everyday rounds.
- Earthquakes, tornadoes, typhoons, fires.

Persons quite naturally ask, "Why do I suffer? I was taught that God is love. But now I wonder—how could a loving God allow this to happen to me?"

Some have become quite angry with God when such events come into their lives. The great Christian writer, C. S. Lewis, wrote about his own grief after the slow and painful death of his wife. He called God a "cosmic sadist," and went on to say,

If God's goodness is inconsistent with hurting us, then either God is not good or there is no God: for in the only life we know

He hurts us beyond our worst fears and beyond all we can imagine. . . . Step by step we were "led up the garden path." Time after time, when He seemed most gracious He was really preparing the next torture.[2]

Who among us hasn't wondered, been hurt, angry, confused by our own undeserved suffering or that of someone we love?

This is yet another question is put to pastors in many forms—still another for which not all the information is in! The classical term for this dilemma is "theodicy." This term comes from Greek and Latin terms meaning "God" and "right." Theodicy is about the righteousness of God in the face of human suffering.

Many a pastor, or other caring friend, has felt himself or herself stumbling in trying to offer anything helpful in the face of such deep and hurting questions. At the same time, we need to remember that not every "Why me?" begs for our answer, or our theological explanations. There is the "rhetorical 'why me?'" The one asking does not expect an answer but is rather looking for permission to think out loud, to express the grief and pain inside in a healing way. Then there is the "companionship 'why me?'" This is similar in that a person may be saying, "I feel so alone and I need to talk. Will you stay with me, be present for me, let me say what I need to, without your imposing your interpretations on me?"[3]

Then, there is certainly a theological "why me?" This is a searching to know where God is and what is God doing in all of this. This question does cry out for a response. Jeffrey Zurheide describes a number of categories of answers that have been given to that question. These answers imply a possible benefit for the sufferer. He notes that each of the following has at least some justification biblically. At the same time, any of these interpretations can be pushed to a sadistic extreme. In my own experience, each of these explanations has some merit if I, the sufferer, claim it for myself. Such interpretations have little value if they are pushed upon me from the outside. At any rate, here are four possible answers to "why me?"

1. The *deterministic* answer: "It's God's will." Some find solace in their suffering, however puzzling it may be that it is all within God's mysterious plan.
2. The *didactic* answer: "God is teaching me something." Some indeed learn, grow, and develop in ways they would not have done

without their suffering. However, this answer must be used with caution. A visitor once asked a person who had just undergone back surgery, "So what is God teaching you through this experience." Responded the patient, "God is teaching me that back surgery hurts like hell!"

3. The *athletic* answer: "My suffering is a training or testing experience from God." Those with this point of view may cite the book of Job, wherein his losses were treated as a sort of cosmic test. Though it's true that life is a test in which one can grow, this view does seem to set God apart from the sufferer.

4. The *disciplinarian* (or punitive) answer: "God uses pain and suffering to punish people for wrongs and sins they committed." Sometimes people carry known guilt. Suffering comes from that source. Other times, people are sure they are being punished, though they are not sure for what.[4]

People use these answers to interpret suffering in human experience, there is yet another side of the issue: What about God? Where is God in all this? Zurheide points to three postulates: God is great; God is good; evil is real. Each of these statements has its basis in Scripture, theology, and experience.

However, some try to solve the mystery of suffering by eliminating one of these three affirmations. For example, some say that evil or suffering is not real. Mary Baker Eddy and Christian Scientists are examples of this. She, and they, contend that God and good are the only realities. Sin and sickness are not good. Therefore sin and sickness are not real. It reminds me of a limerick:

> There was a faith healer of Deal,
> Who said, "Although pain is not real,
> When I sit on a pin
> And it punctures my skin,
> I dislike what I fancy I feel!"[5]

For most of us, this is not a helpful solution.

Others eliminate or challenge the belief that God is good. That is the position, which C. S. Lewis approached when he called God a "cosmic sadist." Lewis pulled back from that position, but others stay there.

Still others try to solve this dilemma by denying God's omnipotence, i.e., the "God is great" statement. On this stance, Zurheide explores Rabbi Harold Kushner's highly acclaimed book, *When Bad Things Happen to Good People.*[6] Kushner struggles compassionately with human suffering including that of his son who died at an early age from progeria (rapid aging). A key part of Kushner's reasoning on this is "there are some things God does not control." Zurheide points to this as a surrender of the "God is great" affirmation. Zurheide suggests that rather than abandoning divine omnipotence, a better approach is to radically *reinterpret* divine omnipotence.[7]

Such a reinterpretation is found in the Gospels. Jesus honored this question of suffering not by providing a systematic answer, but by caring for hurting people, enduring the same dilemmas as we do, and by asking probing questions about it. This may come clear as we consider four questions he asked.

Question one (from Lk 13:2-4): *"Do you think that because these Galileans suffered in this way* [they were beaten and killed by Herod's soldiers] *they were worse sinners. . . . Or those eighteen who were killed when the tower of Siloam fell on them—do you think they were worse offenders?"*

The Galileans, whom Herod's soldiers killed, were taking part in military resistance. Those killed at the tower of Siloam were victims of a construction accident. Are the soldiers who are killed worse sinners than those in the same battle who are not? Are workers injured or killed at work worse sinners than those who are not? Are those who go to work and perish in a terrorist attack worse sinners than those who find an escape, or those not attacked at all?

In other words, is our suffering connected to sin? Is pain connected to personal guilt? He asks us these questions and he gives a simple response, "No." At another point, he answers the same question directly. In John 9, Jesus and his disciples come upon a person blind from birth. This time, the disciples ask him, "Rabbi, who sinned, this man or his parents that he was born blind?" Jesus answers very simply, "Neither." Neither! Not the person himself, nor those who care most about him. Quite clearly, Jesus rejects the disciplinary or punitive interpretation we mentioned earlier.

Whatever may be happening in undeserved suffering, Jesus says, it is *not* connected to guilt. That's good news, because, as we noted, the most universal response when such events happen is either "I wonder what I did to deserve this," or "I *know* what I did to deserve this!" We will need to look further for explanation and understanding.

I believe the nonguilt of the sufferer is what those passages teach. However, in all honesty, it is not quite that neat. In Luke, after Jesus speaks of those killed, he adds, ". . . unless you repent, you will all perish as they did." (It almost sounds like they were only the first of unrepentant sinners to experience tragedy.) In John, Jesus adds that the man was born blind "so that God's works might be revealed in him." (This added sentence could suggest a variety of interpretations.) We must acknowledge the complexity of the passages we cited. Some subthemes deserve further consideration in these Scriptures.

The other three questions all occur within the accounts of Jesus' suffering and death. Question two: *"Am I not to drink the cup that the Father has given me?"* (Jn 18:11). Jesus makes this statement to stop Peter's resistance as Jesus is being arrested in the garden of Gethsemene. Somehow we know that our suffering is connected to Jesus' suffering. Did he deserve what he faced through that painful night and agonizing death on into the next day? If not, why did it happen? I agree with Leslie Weatherhead's perspective in *The Will of God.* On this very point, Weatherhead wrote:

> Was it God's intention from the beginning that Jesus should go to the Cross? I think the answer to that question must be No. I don't think Jesus thought that at the beginning of his ministry. He came with the *intention* that [people] should follow him, not kill him. The discipleship of [people], not the death of Christ, was the intentional will of God. . .
>
> But when the circumstances wrought by [human] evil set up such a dilemma that Christ was compelled either to die or to run away, then *in those circumstances* the Cross was the will of God, but only in those circumstances which were themselves the fruit of evil.[8]

Leslie Weatherhead distinguishes three different aspects of God's will:

1. The *intentional* will of God—God's ideal plan for [humankind].
2. The *circumstantial* will of God—God's plan within certain circumstances.
3. The *ultimate* will of God—God's final realization of [God's] purposes.[9]

Jesus' question about drinking the cup given him is his way of accepting God's *circumstantial* will for him. In this, there is an invitation to consider that whatever our present suffering, it may be God's circumstantial will for us, but we are still in process for what will be God's ultimate will for us.

Jesus' second question leads to the third. It is not addressed to us but to God. We can but reverently listen over his shoulder. Jesus has indeed drunk close to the whole cup given him—he has been arrested, tried, beaten, mocked, and sentenced. He is now agonizing and near death on the cross. He cries out, *"My God, My God, Why have you forsaken me?"* (Mt 27:56). This is the hardest thing we have ever heard Jesus say, the most wrenching and difficult question he has ever asked. Bible scholar James Stalker notes that "In the entire Bible there is no other sentence so difficult to explain."[10]

People try to tone down the terrible agony in that question by pointing out that Jesus was quoting a Psalm, one that begins in despair and ends in triumph. However, that doesn't explain why he picked that verse of that particular Psalm. Somehow it gave voice to the agony he was experiencing.

Scholars have reverently speculated about the accumulation of suffering that stirred this question from Jesus—the rejection of the crowds, the sarcasm of the elite, the hardness of the officials, the cruelty of the soldiers, the fickleness of his followers, the cowardice of his closest friends. However, as Barbara Brown Taylor notes, worst of all was

> the utter silence of God. The God who does not act, the God who is not there. The God who—by a single word—could make all this pain bearable but who did not speak, not so Jesus could hear anyway. . . . The only voice at the end was his own, screaming his last, unanswered question at the sky.[11]

Jesus' question to God also reminds us that we do not suffer alone. As Christians, we believe in God's radical incarnation in the fully human Jesus. In Taylor's words,

> When Jesus howls his question from the cross it is God who howls. . . . Only this is no defeat. This is, contrary to all appearances, a triumph over suffering. By refusing to avoid it or to lie about it in any way, the crucified one opens a way through it.[12]

Though many of us are puzzled by our own suffering, our Christian religion is unique among the religions of the world in proclaiming a God who suffers and who achieves God's redemptive work through this suffering.

This brings us to question four. The cup has now been drunk to its final dregs. It is two days later, the first Easter Sunday. The risen Christ asks this question of Cleopas and his companion, before they recognize who he is. In Luke 24, he asks, *"Was it not necessary that the Messiah should suffer these things and then enter into his glory?"* Through his suffering and death for us and with us, Jesus achieved something that could happen in no other way.

> Not *in spite of* the cross, but *through* the cross, the ultimate aim of God in Christ was achieved as completely as it would have been had [people] followed Christ from the first instead of murdering him. That is why we place the Cross in the very center of what we call God's plan of redemption.
>
> So, in the case of human suffering, God does not will it or desire it, but finally it will not defeat [God] in [God's] plan for the individual sufferer—and [God] has such a plan for each one of us.[13]

Consider the story of Simone Weil. In the 1930s, this young Jewish woman applied for a one-year leave of absence from teaching so that she could work as an unskilled factory laborer and experience those persons' lives. When Hitler occupied France in 1940, she worked as part of the French resistance, eventually migrating to England where she joined the French regime in exile. As a Jew she could not join the struggle officially, but she took part in it. For example, she limited herself to the same rations the occupied French could get with their food cards. She did all this in spite of her education and the privilege and resources that could have been hers. In 1943, sick and malnourished, she entered a hospital and there died, at the age of thirty-four.

Why did she do all this? Because she was a follower of Christ and believed it was possible for one person to take on suffering for the sake of others, and she bet her life on it. She concluded that Christianity has nothing to do with the removal of suffering, no supernatural remedy for suffering. What the Christian faith offers instead is a "supernatural use for suffering."[14]

The same thing is true for each of us. Often through the very suffering we wish we could escape, growth, transformation, renewal, the loving care of God's people, and more happens so that we come out of it different persons, having achieved things and touched lives that would not otherwise be so. None of this is guaranteed, and none of it happens for certain. Yet the mystery remains. Though undeserved suffering would seem to negate the reality of a powerful God of love, many a sufferer knows that is not so.

Someone once wrote, "Pain and sorrow while not God's agents are made God's instruments." A French saying states, "To suffer passes. To have suffered never passes."[15]

In this chapter, I have explored with you the question we all ask, "Why suffering? Why do others suffer? Why do I? How could a loving God allow this to happen?" Our Lord does not directly answer. Instead he leads us into the holy mysteries of suffering, God's, and ours, as he patiently smiles on us and asks, "Is it because of guilt?" (and answers, "No"). He speaks throughout his own horrible ordeal and asks, *"Must I not drink the cup the Father has given me?"* (Must not you?) *"My God, My God, why have you forsaken me?"* (As we hear this, we tremble and then we realize his presence with us in our pain.) Finally, *"Was it not necessary that the Messiah should suffer these things and then enter into his glory?"* (We discover God's transforming power present in what we have suffered.) That is not the whole answer, of course. Instead, it is a series of questions. There is mystery in the questions. But it is not a hollow mystery. Somehow we know that we are not alone in the asking, nor are we alone in the suffering.

Personal Reflection or Group Discussion

1. As an opening experience in a discussion on these matters, you might have different persons read passages from the Bible on suffering. You might include Job 3:1-4, Habakkuk 1:2-4, Psalm 22:1-8. Comment that when we consider suffering we have much company, and then go on to the following questions.

2. Where has mysterious suffering touched your life or those important to you? Make a list of all those occasions you have asked the questions of this chapter. Jot down the thoughts and feelings you had on each occasion.

3. Barbara Brown Taylor notes at times "suffering is a great killer of faith." Was this true for you in the experiences you recalled in question two? Was it for others? How did the suffering affect your faith? How did it affect others' faith?

4. The chapter mentioned that not every "Why me" question wants an answer. Perhaps the person wants a listener instead. Was that true for you when you experienced suffering? What did you want from caring folks at that time?

5. The chapter also points out several different explanations or interpretations as to why suffering occurs. Which of these do you most frequently use when suffering? What seem to you to be the most helpful or satisfying? The least helpful or satisfying?

6. How do Jesus' questions in this regard speak to your problems with undeserved suffering?

7. What other questions of Jesus and what other Bible passages would you add to help you develop your response to undeserved suffering?

Chapter 11

Hope

Our Question:

Where do I find hope?

Jesus' Questions:

Is not life more than food?
Why are you afraid?
And the things you have prepared, whose will they be?
Do you not . . . know I could summon twelve legions of angels?
Did I not tell you that if you believed, you would see the glory of
God?

Scripture: Mt 6:25-34, 8:26, 14:31, 26:53-54; Lk 12:17-20; Jn 11:40.

We humans are storytelling creatures and story-living beings. As we attempt to understand, we do not see isolated, disconnected events. Rather, we perceive events that somehow cohere in a story. It is a story that is still in process; the story is not finished. The story is moving toward some goal, some climax, some conclusion that is important, significant, and hopeful. The future tense is important to us. Whatever we have known in the past and whatever we are experiencing in the present, there is also anticipation of that which will be. This expectation of a better future is described in the single word "hope."

Again and again we are reminded that this expectancy of the future is an important spiritual attribute. For example, philosopher Gabriel Marcel states, "Hope is to the soul what breathing is for the living organism. Where hope is lacking, the soul dries up and withers." Pastoral Counselor Andrew Lester concurs and offers this comment: "The answer to the question, What does it mean to be human? must include our ability to hope. This ability to anticipate the future is . . . perhaps the most authentic and distinctive characteristic of humanity."[1]

Developmental psychologist Erik Erikson believed that hope was the first prerequisite of a person's healthy development. In his view, hope was the necessary foundation for all other human virtues. He wrote, "Hope is both the earliest and the most indispensable virtue inherent in the state of being alive . . . [I]f life is to be sustained hope must remain."[2]

Since hope for the future is so basic, disruption of that hope is devastating. This disruption will happen to most of us, one time or another, because assaults on our future stories come in many ways.

Some of us lose hope for the world. Though the years have dulled the pain of the first shock of September 11, 2001, we all know we live in a fragile, less-secure world, whose future is much more clouded. Media accounts or firsthand encounters with war, poverty, hunger, and ecological devastation cause us to question our assumptions about a durable and dependable world future.

Some of us lose hope for the church. We may have undertaken worthy efforts on behalf of the church, done them with high ideals and the expectation of making a difference, of changing things for the better. Sometimes, though, we see little change, no appreciation, cutback of interest and resources in a cause once dear to us, or petty, endless conflicts. We lose hope.

Some of us lose hope for our lives. We have written treasured scripts about our future story. Then something destroys or disrupts that script. Distraught parents who lost their only child to AIDS, a young adult son, told their pastor, "We have lost our future story." The death of a spouse or a beloved family member seriously alters one's life and expectations. Debilitating disease or destructive habits in oneself or another, divorce, or family problems, may cause one's future story to change. People who expected to be great parents have no children; and those who anticipated being loving grandparents have no grandchildren.

A career does not take off as one hoped, a business fails, a bankruptcy occurs. Things are not unfolding as we anticipated, and our hope wavers to near invisibility.

Then, there are those among us who, for one reason or another, have difficulty constructing a hopeful future story at all. Andrew Lester tells of working with a forty-year-old man named Jason. Jason was referred to this pastoral counselor because of heart symptoms with no discernible physiological basis. In their first interview, they talked about past and present stories with no particular difficulties emerging. Dr. Lester then asked Jason, "What does life look like out in front of you? What stories have you created about the tomorrows?" After a pause, Jason responded, "There won't be many tomorrows." When Dr. Lester urged him to elaborate, Jason explained that his grandfather died of a massive heart attack at age forty-two, and his father had a heart attack and died at age forty-one. From this he concluded that he would be dead in the next year or two. He had no future narrative, no hope.[3]

Other things also cut off hope. A friend of mine told me that the only two older women she knew well—her grandmother and her mother—both had Alzheimer's disease in their eighties. For a time at least, these seemed to be the only models for her future stories of aging—and they held no hope for her.

Whether one has had future stories broken or one has difficulty creating them at all, that person's capacity for hope is in jeopardy. When we cannot hope anymore, we are in despair, a term that originally meant "without hope."

What is despair? In Chapter 5 we explored depression. Despair and depression are similar, but by no means identical. One can be in despair and not have any of the usual symptoms of depression. A despairing person may feel helpless because that person does not believe any activity holds meaning or significance. The hopelessness of despair is more pervasive and universal. It is much more resistant to treatment than depression; a person's worldview has suffered a major breakdown, particularly in regard to the future. Lester notes, ". . . despair may include depressive moods, but despair is primarily related to a cognitive and affective response to philosophical/spiritual problems rooted in or leading to negative perceptions about the future."[4]

A person in despair may withdraw from communities, causes, groups, or activities once cherished. Despair may show up with a defiant question, "What's the use?" Or, it may arise as a wistful questioner softly raises issues he or she doubts can be satisfactorily answered, "Where do I find hope? Why do you hope? After what I have experienced can I ever hope again, and if so, where is the way? What is the ground for hoping?" It is a fascinating experience to bring this contemporary search to the Christian Scriptures. We discover that both the term and the concept "hope" is a central theme in the latter part of the New Testament. Suprisingly, the term "hope" is hardly mentioned in the Gospels, and yet at the same time we find that Jesus lived in confident, hopeful trust in a God at work in his life and in the world. So let us bring our questions about finding hope and see what happens in a dialogue with Jesus' questions of us.

Jesus' first question to us is really a series of rhetorical questions that he offered in a portion of the "Sermon on the Mount." *"Is not life more than food, and the body more than clothing? . . . And can any of you by worrying add a single hour to your span of life? . . . And why do you worry about clothing? . . . But if God so clothes the grass of the field which is alive today and tomorrow is thrown into the oven, will he not much more clothe you—you of little faith?"* (Mt 6:25b-30).

In this passage, Jesus alternates between telling the hearers important truths about God's providence and care and inviting persons through questions to identify and claim those same truths for themselves. *Is not life more than food?* (Of course). Have you not experienced that which is more than food? Did not God give you life? If God performed the miracle of creating life in you, is not God capable of providing what you need for that life to be sustained? Furthermore, does not your experience prove this to be true? Are you not alive to this day because God has provided for you? Is not your life the richer because God has also given you that which is more than food and clothing? This first set of queries opens our eyes to all God has already provided to stimulate our trustful hope.

Jesus' next questions expand upon this truth because these are asked confrontively in more dire circumstances. Again, the question is asked in a series of similar events. In one instance, frightened disciples awaken Jesus as their boat is being swamped in a sudden storm. Jesus asks, *"Why are you afraid, you of little faith?"* (Mt 8:26). Then, at his word, the lake is calmed. Later, again in a storm on the lake, Jesus walks toward them. Peter begs permission to come to Jesus on the waves and starts out. Then he "noticed the strong wind . . . became frightened" and as he sank cried out for help. Jesus again rescues him, and then asks, *"You of little faith, why did you doubt?"* (Mt 14:31). If these questions seem harsh, we need to hear what Jesus is saying. He is telling the disciples and us to learn from experience! Did we not hear his gentle questions in Matthew 6, and did not our hearts respond with assent and remembrance that God's care and provision are true? Were we not asked to apply this experience to our fright in the lake storm? Was not Peter expected to remember both of these events when he wanted to take a new step in faith? God gave us a memory—use it! Let past experiences of God's care give us perspective on our present perplexities and hope for the future. Paul Zahl comments, "Hope is remembrance projected on the future. It satisfies because it is based on an objective past."[5] For us, this past includes the entire Jesus story plus our own experience of God's grace and provision. This can change us and give us perspective as we face new episodes of future stories under attack.

Jesus' great follower, Paul, made this discovery when he wrote, "we boast [or rejoice] in our sufferings, knowing that suffering produces endurance, and endurance produces character, and character produces hope, and hope does not disappoint us, because God's love has been poured into our hearts through the Holy Spirit that has been given to us" (Rom 5:3-5). God's grace, which had encountered Paul in his misguidedness and saved him, had also sustained him through great difficulties and suffering. Out of all that, Paul experienced a hope, a hope that did not disappoint him. He not only claimed it for the past but also took hold of it to face all future suffering that might come. Jesus' second set of questions guides us to discover what we have learned, to claim those assurances, and to hold on to them in times of despair.

We move on to another question Jesus asked. *"And the things you have prepared, whose will they be?"* (Lk 12:20). This question occurs in a parable Jesus told. As Luke describes it, the occasion was Jesus' refusal to enter into a family conflict over inheritance. As Jesus refuses, he tells them a story of a rich man who prospers so much that he has nowhere to store his crops. The rich man decides to build bigger storage barns and then states, "Soul, you have ample goods laid up for many years; relax, eat, drink, be merry." This sounds harmless enough; as a matter of fact, it seems a quite contemporary image of retirement.

Jesus does not see it that way. He puts the evaluation of this man's decision into the voice of God who calls him fool, and tells him that this very night his life would be demanded of him. Then God asks—"And the things you have prepared, whose will they be?" If there is any doubt as to the meaning of this parable with its searching question, note this sentence, "So it is with those who store up treasures for themselves but are not rich toward God" (Lk 12:21).

The question might be put this way: Is your future story too small, too confined, perhaps limited to yourself and your own welfare or of those close to you? (Too small hopes will fail you, and they should!) Do you need a broader, deeper, grander hope? Andrew Lester speaks of "finite hope" and of "transfinite hope." Finite hope is placed in physiological sensing and the material world. Transfinite hope goes beyond that to embrace "the mystery and the excitement of open-ended future and the not-yet."[6] Finite hope might be the self-centered preoccupation described in Jesus' parable, or it might be broadened to include these same blessings of peace and prosperity for a larger group. Transfinite hope is willing to be mystified, uncertain, incomplete, with the trust that one is within the vast and mysterious stories of God.

How does this help us with our question, "Where do I find hope?"? Our hope may be dashed because our future story was too small and confining. Paradoxically, hope may be rekindled by hoping "transfinitely!" As Martin Luther King Jr., who lived with many setbacks and much suffering, once said, "We must accept finite disappointment, but we must never lose infinite hope."[7] Perhaps this is one of the solemn questions in the years following September 11, 2001: Was our world too small, and thus our hope for the world too limited and confining? May it be that out of this pain and outrage, our commitment to global justice, and our hope for it, is born anew.

For those of us who have despaired of the church—what do Jesus' questions indicate? Could there be a call to a chastened, smaller perhaps, but realistic hope that God has yet more to say through this very human instrument that is entrusted with divine mission?

This brings us to a final pair of Jesus' questions. He asks one of them as he is being arrested in the Garden of Gethsemene. After Judas' betraying kiss, another disciple swings out with a sword. Jesus tells him to put the sword back and then asks, *"Do you not think I can appeal to my Father, and he will at once send me more than twelve legions of angels?"* (Mt 26:53). He goes on to ask, how would the Scriptures be fulfilled? His disciples saw themselves as twelve outnumbered, overwhelmed, defeated persons, unable to prevent the tragedy that was about to take place. In contrast, Jesus saw unlimited resources, twelve powerful legions of fiery angels, to prevent this capture, or, to sustain him in it, which is the course he chose.

This pairs with a question that the Gospel of John reports as Jesus stood outside the tomb of his late, dear friend Lazarus. On the fourth day after Lazarus' death, Jesus commands that the tomb be opened.

When Martha objects, Jesus' asks, *"Did I not tell you that if you believed, you would see the glory of God?"* (Jn 11:40).

Jesus asked both of these questions in the process of undergoing that on which sturdy New Testament hope is built—his passion, suffering, death, and resurrection. This is a story in which the hope of his dearest friends was cruelly shattered. Then, not only were those shattered hopes gloriously restored, they were given eyes to see that hopelessness never need be the last word again! In the mysterious love of God, seen in the face of the crucified and risen Christ, there is always another way and one more story to be told.

As William Barclay once wrote, "The Christian hope is not simply a trembling, hesitant hope that perhaps the promises of God may be true. It is the confident expectation that they cannot be anything else than true."[8]

How does all this help any of us who find our hope wavering? Perhaps the following will help us connect this New Testament story to our story. William Lynch noted that the path to healing for some people stricken by mental illness was to imagine a world different from the one in which they are imprisoned. In a similar vein, the poet Hugh Kenner wrote, "Whoever can give his people better stories than the ones they live in is like the priest in whose hands common bread and wine become capable of feeding the very soul."[9]

A way to find hope, therefore, is to find better stories that portray a different world than the one we live in. We have noted how the Jesus story provides searching questions and just such an alternative, triumphant story. Gifted counselors learn from this and invite alternative stories as well. This was how Andrew Lester helped his counselee Jason, who believed he would soon die of a heart attack. He helped him create a more hopeful future story by asking him to draw a genogram of his genetic heritage. He was able to see that in his genes were also people who had lived long, healthy lives. Jason was also encouraged to compare his lifestyle to that of his father and grandfather, and he discovered he was living much more wisely. Gradually, he came to believe that he had a future story.

At a time when my view of the world had become jaded and clouds of despair hovered in my sky, hope was reborn with the birth of a child, my very first grandchild. The moment he was born, I began to care more deeply about the future of a world in which he would live. My love for him and his love for me, his joy and delight in discovering this world made it anew a place of wonder for me. I lived in a new and better story, and my hope was revived.

My friend who dreaded old age also found a different future story in which to hope. She met, befriended, and came to admire older persons who modeled for her aging with vigor, integrity, and hope. With the help of these more positive images, she told me, "I wrote a statement about the woman I want to be at age eighty. We gravitate toward what we see in our mind's eye. I tried on a mental image and now I live toward it."

This calls to mind the story of Pablo Picasso, who, years ago, was asked to paint the portrait of a young poet, Gertrude Stein. When, after months of work, he unveiled the painting, people were shocked. For Picasso had drawn her not as the young, uncertain woman that most people saw her, but rather as old, wise, and strong. When his fellow artists objected, "But that doesn't look like her," he responded, "It will one day." Joan Delaplane concludes, "And, in truth, it happened. The artist had a vision of what she would look like and be one day and framed the vision in his own famous portrait."[10]

These stories describe imaginative, creative people engendering hope in themselves and in others. For make no mistake, imagination, creativity, and a new story do indeed call forth hope. Hope may also be found in groups and communities of persons who claim their stories and share them with one another. In such groups, we learn that hope is a sense of the possible, the sense that life is open-ended, and filled with possibilities, even though we may have to let go of some of our future stories.

The most basic source of the better stories than the ones in which we live is the New Testament. The New Testament is witness to the one who overcame all the powers of darkness and death, who came to bring life full of joy and promise and hope. Jesus' questions to us have made us aware how rich this heritage of hope truly is. Jesus died and rose again, giving us hope as we come to grips with our own dying. (We will explore hope in the face of death in more detail in the next chapter.)

We have asked where we find hope when we lose it. Our leader's probing questions remind us not to set our hope on things too small. Rather, the questions invite us to recall God's gracious provision, to learn and grow from that, and to live with the whole Gospel story until our hope is so big and grand, it is couched in wonder and mystery.

Personal Reflection or Group Discussion

1. Here is a possible beginning activity: In the movie *South Pacific*, Nurse Nellie Forbush sings about being a "cockeyed optimist" and proclaims "I'm stuck like a dope with a thing called hope and I can't get it out of my heart." Invite people to recall the folks they have known who were "cockeyed optimists"—always hopeful and upbeat. Have them tell one story about such persons.
2. What are your biggest challenges to remaining a hopeful person?
3. What keeps you hoping in spite of those challenges?
4. What future stories have been broken or disrupted for you? What did you do to reconstruct them?
5. Which of the questions from Jesus spoke to you in your search for hope? In what ways?
6. What other Scripture passages inform you and inspire you to hope?

Chapter 12

Death and Grief

Our Questions:

What happens when I die?
What can I do about the pain of grief?

Jesus' Questions:

Whom are you looking for?
Woman, why are you weeping?
I am the resurrection and the life. . . . Do you believe this?
If it were not so, would I have told you that I go to prepare a
place for you?

Scripture: Jn 11:1-44, 14:1-7, 20:1-18

Every one of us lives with two dreads and two griefs—that we will lose persons important in our life, and that our own lives will end. We also live in a society that frequently denies and ignores these important truths about death. Both women and men are offered a variety of cosmetics and surgical procedures to make us appear young and youthful as though we will live endlessly. We do not make death part of our daily thinking or conversation. When someone dies, we relegate this significant event to the hospital and the funeral home. We then give it as little attention as possible and urge the mourners to get over it as soon as possible. Death is avoided, feared, and denied in our society. Furthermore, we benefit from technology that has done wonderful things in extending life. When the twentieth century dawned, fourteen out of every 100 infants died in the first year of life. As the twenty-first century dawns, the statistic is less than fourteen in every 1,000. In 1900, half of all parents with three children would see one of them die before age fifteen. Today, that probability is 6 percent.

A century ago, life expectancy was about fifty years. Today, it has increased by 60 percent to about eighty. Almost certainly, this life expectancy will increase even more in the years to come. "Futurist" Russell Chandler points out that half of all Americans who have ever lived past the age of sixty-five are alive right now. The fastest growing age segment in this country is those older than eighty-five.[1]

However, marvelous technology and wonderful progress do not always succeed. Accident and illness threaten at every stage of life. Still, we lose people we love along the way. Even if we live to be 100, the mortality rate on this earth is still 100 percent.

Deep within ourselves we know this all too well. As Howard Clinebell, the late pastoral counseling professor, once noted, almost every church is a cauldron of unresolved grief. In every neighborhood, people's hearts are breaking. Some grieve recent deaths. Others hurt from losses that occurred long ago, but somehow they are blocked from a full release through grieving. Still others are concerned about people they love whose health is fragile. All of us have equal concerns about ourselves. We ask, "How can I mourn healthily? What can I do about the pain of grief? How can I die with dignity? What happens when I die?"

For those with such burdens, Jesus comes to us as both question and answer. He lived with full awareness and candor about his own imminent death. Jesus also vividly discussed the power of God in, through, and beyond death. Furthermore, our Lord raised penetrating questions in this realm, questions that push us beyond our shallow denial to the vast implications of a faith, deeply held. As we enter this dialogue, we will first explore part of the Resurrection story in the Gospel of John. Then we will look at two more passages in John that both anticipate and fill in more detail as to what Christ's resurrection means to us. Out of this, we will examine four probing questions from Jesus.

In John 20, we see people who are candidates for what is now called "complicated" or "pathological" grief, that is grief from which people have tremendous difficulty recovering, if they ever do. They have lost so much. They have lost the one on whom they depended at a young age, lost him to a violent, unnecessary, and sudden death, lost their hope for the future, lost their companion, friend, encourager, lost their purpose for living. In short, they lost the person they loved with their whole being, the one on whom they had bet their lives.

At the beginning of John 20, Mary Magdalene has come to the grave of Jesus very early in the morning, while it was still dark. In those days, it was believed that the dead person's spirit hovered around the tomb for three or four days, and so perhaps she hoped for one more glimmer of presence or some small message before all was silent.

Although some traditions have made Mary Magdalene the prostitute who washed Jesus' feet with her tears in Luke 7, Scripture gives us no evidence for that. Rather, the Bible tells us that Jesus healed her of "seven demons"—probably a reference to how severe and recurrent her illness had been. She responded with wholehearted devotion to Jesus and his cause. Mary Magdalene was among those who traveled with him and contributed financially. She was part of his band of followers on that final trip to Jerusalem. She was one of the few followers who stayed with him at his crucifixion and was among those who saw where Jesus was entombed what was left of him. This woman was a devoted friend and follower to the very end. Out of such loving, she was one of those hurt most by his cruel death.

When she came in that early darkness, there was one more outrage, "the stone had been removed from the tomb." In dismay, she ran and told the disciples. Two of them in turn came running. One looked from the outside, and one went in and investigated, seeing the piles of grave clothes. With dawning awareness, they left.

As Barbara Brown Taylor notes, the rest of this story in John 20 belongs to Mary.[2] With eyes still clouded by weeping, she bent over and peered in the tomb. Even the presence of angels did not comfort her. Their question was *"Woman, why are you weeping?"* So imprisoned by her grief was she that it did not occur that they might have light and comfort to give. (Grief can do that—block out all comfort and reassurance others might have to offer.) With deadness in her speech, she replied, "They have taken away my Lord, and I do not know where they have laid him."

She walked a few steps away, her grief-dimmed eyes still focused on that violated tomb. Another person spoke. This presence also asked, *"Woman, why are you weeping?"* It continued, *"Whom are you looking for?"*

She thought she was talking to the gardener, and so she said, "Sir, if you have carried him away, tell me where you have laid him, and I will take him away." Then this supposed gardener spoke to her by

name, not only that, the most intimate form of her name, "Mariam."
This was the way Jesus had always said her name. It startled her into
awareness, that wonder of wonders, somehow she was once again in
personal relationship with the one who had loved her so lavishly and
she had loved so faithfully. She had hoped for the tiniest glimmer,
some hint of his spirit. Instead, she was given a radiant, powerful
presence. Mary's response is total. "She turned to him. . .", turned
from staring into a tomb with teary eyes, turned from looking *away* to
looking *at* him, a person, a gift, so much more than she ever could
have hoped.

With an exclamation of worship, she bowed before him and called
out "Rabboni"—a term of address that has a higher significance than
the ordinary word, "rabbi."[3] She was also about to throw her arms
around him for sheer joy and wonder. But he stopped her.[4] Even as
she reached out to hug him around the knees, he spoke a word that
must have hurt and puzzled her, at least a little. Various Bible translations communicate Jesus' words, "Touch me not" or "Do not hold on
to me" or perhaps more accurately, "Do not cling to me." Mary, I am
alive and powerful, but our relationship will have to change. No longer can I be a hand to hold physically when the going gets tough, or a
shoulder to lean on, or a breast to weep on. Rather, I will be alive inside your life, renewing, restoring, guiding, and empowering. Mary,
your first responsibility is to be this "go to my brothers and say to
them 'I am ascending to my Father and your Father, to my God and
your God.'"[5]

So Mary did just that. She returned to where the disciples were
hovering. "'I have seen the Lord,' she said and whatever dark doubts
they might have had on the subject earlier, one look at her face was
enough to melt them all away like morning mist."[6] That is the beautiful story that John 20 tells.

In light of that story, consider the questions we ask and the ones Jesus asks. We began by asking, "What happens when I die?" Scripture
reminds us that that is a mystery. Scripture doesn't even tell us what
happened when Jesus died.

Barbara Brown Taylor aptly notes that Jesus' resurrection was an
event that was entirely between him and God. The Bible speaks of no
witnesses at all. Since no one was there, no one can say what actually
happened inside that tomb on that Sunday morning. Disciples and

friends arrived after the fact and saw only the artifacts, clothes, and angels. The vast majority saw nothing at all because they were still in bed.[7]

There was an empty tomb, but the empty tomb was not the point.

We struggle with the promise of resurrection because it doesn't seem to square with anything else we know about human life. No one has ever seen it happen. But then, remember, no one saw it happen that first Easter, either. All that we know of this mystery is that it is somehow connected to us. "Because I live, you also will live," Jesus promised (Jn 14:19). We have come to know this Jesus as one who keeps his promises.

Part of the answer to our question lies in joyous mystery, to which we can only point with symbols. The rainbow is a symbol of resurrection, a reminder of God's promises. The Easter lily is a symbol of a dead, dry bulb that grows to great beauty. The butterfly is a reminder of God's promise of resurrection. I love the story of the two caterpillars walking along the ground. They looked up at a lovely butterfly, soaring and zigzagging crazily all over with great freedom and joy. Said one caterpillar to the other, "You'll never get me up in one of those things." But that caterpillar will, and so will you and I. We will be changed from one glory into another, that resurrection we share with Jesus, and mysteriously we will soar into the very presence of our loving Lord.

This brings us to the first two questions Jesus asked. He asked these questions of Mary Magdalene within the passage we just related. One was *"Whom are you looking for?"*

Barbara Brown Taylor tells that as a child, she loved to spend time in the woods looking for treasures. One of her favorite treasures was a cicada shell, one of those dry, brown bug bodies you find on tree trunks when the seventeen-year locusts come out of the ground. She liked them because they were horrible looking with their huge empty eye sockets and all, and she could frighten the timid children with them. She liked them also because they were evidence that a miracle had occurred. They looked dead, but weren't, as they were just shells. There was a neat slit down the back of each shell, where the living creature had escaped.

Bringing that childhood experience the Easter story, Taylor reminds us, "The tomb was just the cicada shell with the neat slit down its back. The living being that had once been inside it was gone."[8] The encounters, the wonder, the rejoicing, and more was going on somewhere else. This may be the reason that most who came to the tomb did not stay very long.

Jesus, the risen one, had outgrown his tomb. That was far too small a focus for the resurrection. Rather, he had people to see and things to do. His very first encounter was with Mary, and his question stirs in her awareness where not to look and where she should look.

At this point, there is a playful turn in the story. In an account as solemn as a resurrection story, you would not expect to find something like child's play. Mary was looking for someone, and never found him. Rather, like a game of hide-and-seek or blindman's bluff, Jesus found Mary! In the twentieth and twenty-first chapters of John, the risen Christ has five experiences in which he finds friends, and comes to them with words of comfort, commissioning, and hope. "Every time he came to his friends they became stronger, wiser, kinder, more daring. Every time he came to them, they became more like him."[9] This is where resurrection begins, not in the tomb, but in their encounters with the living Lord, and with our encounters as well, in whatever manner these may occur.

As we live with our mortality and grief, as we look for something or someone to help us with our dread, there is One looking for us, asking, *"Whom are you looking for?"* Like Mary, we may not find him as we expect. Rather we learn that we are found by a friend who promises to stand by us through all eternity!

The second question Jesus asked Mary and us is, *"Why are you weeping?"* The answer seems obvious. Mary was weeping because she had lost her best friend to death and then believed his body to be violated. We, too, weep for many reasons.

Certainly Jesus is not asking us to end all weeping. As someone wisely wrote, "Tears are the soap of the soul, cleansing us from the clinging grime of grief or guilt."[10] Even as people of hope, sometimes the tears will come, and tears are okay, even welcome. (In my opinion, many of us males need to cry more freely and discover for ourselves the power of tears to release the pain inside.) We may weep because of our failures, our disappointments, our frustrations, or even our joys. We cry because we miss someone who has died, and perhaps we shed tears because we remember and too few others still do. We may cry because we feel guilty or angry, or because we have unfinished business with the one that died.

Counselors talk about "grief work," that is, going through the difficult process of accepting a death, experiencing all the emotions that go with that acknowledgment, and finding ways to fill the holes that person's death left. Jesus affirms such mourning. He promised us, "Blessed are those who mourn, for they shall be comforted" (Mt 5:4). We are told that "Jesus wept," or in the New Revised Standard Version, "Jesus began to weep" (Jn 11:35). One counselor translates it "Jesus weeps." Indeed, Jesus enters into our suffering and loss out of his rich knowledge of such grief.

Tears can be wholesome—if we grieve as persons of hope rather than persons of despair. However, if they are our only and dominant mood, perhaps we are still living in the gloom of Jesus' death rather than in the light of Jesus' resurrection.

After we have shed our tears, a time comes to commend ourselves and our loved ones to the care of our loving God who raised Jesus from the dead and who promised that one day, God will wipe all tears from our eyes. That one day, we will be brought to a place where there shall be no more death, no mourning nor crying, nor pain, for the former things have passed away.

Jesus asked of Mary and us, "Why are [we] weeping?" Are our tears expressions of letting go? Or are those tears signs that we have not let go and still cannot?

As beautiful and important as these questions are, there are two other questions that also invite our consideration. They are closely related in meaning and significance. Jesus asked one of these questions when he came to Martha and Mary after their brother (and his good friend) Lazarus had died. Martha expressed regret that Jesus had not come sooner. Jesus promised that her brother would rise again. Martha responded with orthodox belief that he would so on the last day. Then Jesus made a powerful statement and followed it with a question. *"I am the resurrection and the life. Those who believe in me, even though they die, will live, and everyone who lives and believes in me will never die. Do you believe this?"* (Jn 11:25-26).

Again, Barbara Brown Taylor captures the meaning and power of what Jesus said:

> He does not say he has the power to give resurrection and life. He says that he *is* those things, that in his presence they become present reality, because he is one with the Great I Am whose life is indestructible. Those who hook up with him will never die, no matter what happens to their bodies, because he is hooked up with the source and sustainer of all life. Those who trust that

with him—in him—begin their eternal lives right now and nothing on earth can snuff them out.[11]

Jesus does indeed make this awesome claim, promise, and invitation: Believe in me, die to your old self, and you will never die again. Then he asks his question, "Do you believe this?" or perhaps more accurately, "Do you trust this?"

We ask, "What happens when I die?" Jesus responds that when we trust in him and his promises, our death is a minor incident in our continuing life with him. We ask "What can I do about the pain of grief?" Jesus allows and enters into all the loneliness that is ours for a while but then calls upon us to see that both the one who died and we are in the hands of the same loving God. But then he asks, "Do you believe in this and trust in it?" We will never be asked a more important question. The way we answer will influence not only how we view death and how we grieve but everything else as well.

This question is closely related to the fourth and final question we will consider on this subject. Jesus asks it in John 14, in the middle of what is often called Jesus' "farewell discourses" with his disciples. As he prepares them for his death, he tells them not to let their hearts be troubled, to believe in God and him. Then he makes a profound promise that has been variously translated: "In my father's house are many mansions/rooms/dwelling places/places to abide" (Jn 14:2a). Then comes his question, *"If it were not so, would I have told you that I go to prepare a place for you?"* The meaning of this verse and this question turn on two key issues: What is the meaning of that word variously translated mansion, room, abiding place; and, where are those places? Sensitive scholars have noted that this verse is not only a promise about persons who died. God's abiding places—places to be in relationship, to feel parental love and care, to be renewed and restored—such places abound, in this life and the next. If one interprets the text this way, the verse assures us that what we know of relationship with God in this life informs us about the next. Then Jesus adds his challenging question: *"If this were not true, would I be boldly going ahead of you to prepare new places for you?"* The fitting response is, "Of course not, of course the promise is true." The question also challenges. If the promise is true, live it, claim it, trust it. There are indeed abiding places in this life and the next. Though we see it dimly, we *do* see it. These questions stir our more profound believing and our deeper trusting. Research has been done with people who either had near-death experiences or were clinically dead and revived. That gives partial and preliminary witness to what we have discussed here. Raymond Moody, in his book, *Life After Life,* reports on hundreds of interviews with such people. Although there is much variety in these experiences, a frequent, common element in these near-death experiences was an encounter with a very bright light. People sensed that this light was a personal being and felt love and warmth emanating from it. The dying individuals often felt surrounded by the light, at peace with it, and accepted. The people were drawn to the light as to an irresistible magnet.[12]

I have known two persons who had such experiences. One was my dear friend, David Johnson. Shortly before I met him, in his early thirties, Dave had a severe heart attack. For days he hovered between life and death. One day, he had a vivid awareness of lying in a room in which there was a window with billowing white curtains, beyond which was a bright light. The light grew brighter and brighter, and Dave felt his bed moving toward it, indeed as if drawn by a magnet. He felt at peace and eager to go to the light. After a time, he experienced the light dimming and his bed receding away from the window, and Dave realized he could not go there at that time. Though he had a wife and two young children he loved greatly, he confessed that at that moment he felt disappointed. Dave lived for about twenty-five years after that. His vivid sense that life was a temporary trust to savor and that death was nothing to fear never left him. The other person was the man who was president of my theological school when I was a student there. His name was Dr. Herbert Gezork. I admired Dr. Gezork's dynamic leadership and powerful, insightful sermons during my days of learning in seminary, and I was touched to read about how he died. After he retired, he moved to Florida to live out his last years. While there, he became very ill and was taken to the hospital for the last time. His pastor was with him at the end. As his life was slipping away, Dr. Gezork's last words were "It's more beautiful than anything I ever dreamed."[13]

On this topic of death, Jesus has spoken more times, lived the issue with his own life, and asked more probing questions than any other question we asked. We have said what we can about that manifold witness, and yet it is still a mystery. Death is another of those areas where not all the information is in, nor will it be within this lifetime. But it is a holy mystery, a gracious and loving mystery. With Martha we learn to trust the mystery, to believe now, to live gratefully, all the while anticipating the greater glory to be revealed.

Personal Reflection or Group Discussion

1. Invite the group to divide into smaller groups of three or four. Invite everyone to finish any one of these sentences, and then elaborate just a bit:
   a. Of all the people I've known, the person most courageous about his or her own death was . . .
   b. The most unforgettable funeral or memorial service I ever attended was . . .
   c. The most helpful advice I ever heard on the subject of death and grieving is . . . (also make it clear that it is okay to pass if a person does not wish to speak on these things.)
2. What are the greatest losses in your life? What are the most recent losses?
3. In regard to those losses, how do you feel you are doing with your "grief work", i.e., accepting the loss, expressing your feelings about it, finding ways to cope with the loss, and living with change? What do you need to help you do even better?
4. What are your feelings about your own mortality? About the mortality of people you love?
5. Have you had a near-death experience such as those in the chapter? Have you known anyone who has? If so, how does this affect one's view of and attitude toward death?
6. In what ways did the Scripture passages and questions discussed in this chapter speak to your concerns?
7. What other Bible passages or questions of Jesus would you add to this discussion?

Epilogue

Asked and Unasked Questions

In this book, I have reported the questions my pastoral staff and I garnered as we listened carefully for a period of time to persons in the congregation we served. This is a Midwestern suburban church made up of mostly European Americans of reasonably comfortable means. For about three months, we listened intently, gathering the questions for the series that became this book. I also reflected on this list with my pastoral counselors support group and added a question or two from concerns they heard most urgently or consistently.

Responding to these questions was a fascinating discipline. At times, it felt rather like a school assignment—working on topics assigned to me, rather than those of my own choosing. This task was like exploring a different kind of lectionary, part of it Scripture and part of it the "living human document." It led me to study and reflect on some topics I had never considered before. At other times, I found myself tempted to stick my questions in rather than those assigned, because, of course, my questions were most pressing to me. In the end, I grew from keeping faith with this discipline, and I trust the first readers and hearers did as well.

The dialogue with Jesus' questions was tantalizing to me at the beginning of this work, and that dialogue grew on me as I went on. It led me to explore some aspects of each topic rather than others. Most basically, it helped avoid what Rowan Williams has called, "the great lie of religion: the god who fits our agenda."[1] God is not removed from our pain, struggles, questions, but is also other, more, and greater than those struggles. This method helped me remember that.

In retrospect, I find it important to think about our method of gathering these questions, and therefore of the nature of the questions we heard. I did not advertise in church publications and ask people to submit questions. Nor did I make an announcement from the pulpit or put a questionnaire in the church bulletin. Our method was quiet and subtle. We listened for those queries that occurred in the midst of our other pastoral activities, conversing, calling, counseling, teaching, preaching, and listening. These questions are therefore a small slice, a cross section of concerns of a group of people; this was from a certain time in the life of one church. I have gone on to report and respond on this set of questions, because it felt to me that they spoke of widespread feelings and needs, a worthy collection crying out for caring pastoral response.

I also find myself reflecting about the questions no one asked us, the items that were not on this list. I think some of the unasked questions just did not come up at this time. Other questions of great importance may not occur to people, or may be explored in other settings but not with their pastors. Quite possibly, there are questions of great importance that people do not ask at all. At any rate, here are some of the questions we were not asked.

Though there were a number of questions about parenting, no one asked us a question about marriage. Yet statistics clearly show that marriage is in a troubled state. Those who care about people know that in early, middle, and late years of marriage, there are many issues that need to be faced, skills to be learned, and recommitments to be made if a marriage is to survive and thrive. Yet for some reason, we were not asked.

During this time, there were no questions about domestic abuse or violence—physical, mental, spiritual, or sexual. As pastor, I mentioned the subject of such violence in a sermon every several months, suggesting that it could be faced, dealt with, and overcome. From time to time, people would respond and ask for help working on such matters.

There were no questions about obsessive, or addictive behavior problems, e.g., alcohol, nicotine, other drugs, food, sex, work. Certainly such problems are present in any group of people these days. At the very least, a pastor needs to be aware of the best available community resources to which to refer those needing such support. With increasing frequency, I am hearing of men being hooked by too-easy access to pornography and sexual conversations on the Internet—a new twist to an age-old issue. However, during this time, people did not ask about this range of troubling issues.

Nor were there any questions about the two sexual/ethical questions about which the Christian church seems to be polarizing—abortion and homosexuality. This is in spite of the fact that people have had to deal with decisions around abortion, and church members do have beloved family members who are homosexual. I fear people have taken the measure of the church on these topics and have concluded they will only hear a vigorous ideological argument on one side or the other, not compassionate listening and care. So they work out these dilemmas for themselves, thank you.

We did not hear questions about "macro" issues. People did not ask for ethical perspectives on directions of our government. They did not ask for Christian prophetic perspective on the arms race, or Christian response to terrorism, or the growing gap between rich and poor, or ways to combat the lingering racism in our culture, or for perspectives on the gun-control debate. No one asked for Christian perspective on ecological and environmental issues. No one raised questions about the morality of the corporation or organization for which they worked. This is in spite of a profoundly corporate emphasis within Scriptures and of many important Christian leaders since.

Martin Luther King Jr. reminded us that, "Religion that ends with the individual, ends." Ethicist Ronald Stone adds, "No matter how scrupulous one is, if a corporate structure or a government policy assists some employees of a firm in becoming rich while others are kept poor, stealing has occurred."[2] Still, questions are rarely, if ever, raised about corporate responsibilities. We seem to concentrate more on the personal and the private.

Now, let us turn to the questions that *were* asked. As I attempted to give some structure to the questions I did hear, I separated them into questions about finding our way and questions about God's way with us. One person suggested that there was a fourfold division in these questions: (1) What are the values by which we will live? (2) What are the resources to sustain us in those values? (3) What is the content of the faith that is the source of value and strength? (4) How do we engage that faith?

These are helpful ways of organizing these queries, but in a certain sense, they defied organization. I believe it was Carl Jung who once noted that when people came to him with a sexual problem, it turned out to be a theological one, and if they came to him with a theological problem, it turned out to be a sexual one! In a similar way, questions that appeared to be strictly personal were spiritual and theological, and the theological questions had a connection to deep personal longing and need.

In further reflecting on the questions that were asked and those that were not, I am reminded of Abraham Maslow's "hierarchy of needs."

Maslow constructed a several-layer pyramid of needs. He believed that the most basic needs had to be satisfied before a person could go on and consider the "higher" needs.

Following are these needs, moving from most basic to more complex, as Maslow saw them.

1. The need for *survival*—surviving danger, hunger, cold, lack of housing.
2. The need for *safety*—guarding against the loss of what is important to a person, what a person holds dear.
3. The need for *love* and affection—intimacy, belonging, being considered enjoyable and worthy of love.
4. The need for *esteem*—the sense of being accepted, respected, held in high regard by our peers.
5. The need for *self-actualization*—the desire to become everything we are meant to be.

These constituted Maslow's original pyramid or hierarchy of values. In his later years, Maslow added two more needs:

6. The need to *understand*—to see life and understand it, to find God and first causes.
7. The creative need for *beauty,* music, art, literature, or whatever speaks to an individual's aesthetic need.[3]

As I look at the questions raised with us through this lens, I realize that they run the gamut of basic human needs of which Maslow spoke—survival, safety, love, esteem, self-actualization, understanding, and beauty.

Out of these reflections, I draw three conclusions.

First, it is a faithful exercise for a pastor to respond to the questions people ask. I believe it was Gandhi who once said that God dare not appear to a hungry person save as a piece of bread. In other words, faith and theology touches a person at that person's most basic need or not at all. Whatever our questions, whatever our starting place, pastors should be there to respond.

Second, pastors need to do more, say more than respond to the questions asked them. In my experience, the gaps represented by the unasked questions are vast. Some of the unasked questions cry out for a caring discussion that will end the uneasy silence. Some of the unasked questions imply a faulty and partial understanding of what the fullness of Christian discipleship is. So, in addition to responding to the questions pastors are asked, they are called to raise the questions no one asks them. An educative question increases awareness and opens doors. Though this may be a difficult and uncomfortable task, nevertheless, asking those tough, educative questions is part of the pastor's calling.

Third, though it is beyond the scope of this book, I am confident that the method we have engaged thus far would enlighten other types of questions we have mentioned in this chapter. For each of our questions, our Lord's bold presence and probing questions would yield insight, awareness, depth, or perspective. In all this there is at least the beginning of a way for a disciple to live in obedience.

For now, our opportunity is to reflect and act on what we have thus far discovered and to rejoice in the one who became "like his brothers and sisters in every respect, so that he might be a merciful and high priest in the service of God. . ." (Heb 2:17).

Personal Reflection or Group Discussion

1. For an opening exercise, invite people to browse the table of contents and first part of this chapter to locate the one or two most important questions for them as they attempt to be disciples of Christ.
2. What questions are important to you that are neither in the table of contents or in this chapter? What strategy do you have for gaining perspectives on these questions?
3. In your opinion, how effective is the strategy of this book, that is, linking our questions to the questions of Jesus? How could this method have better met your need? What other Bible study methods would you employ to address these questions?
4. What discoveries and insights have you made as you went through this book and this process? What have you been called to see differently or do differently?
5. As you complete this study, what would you like to explore next? What is your plan for carrying on this investigation?

Appendix A

Jesus' Questions in the Synoptic Gospels

(*Note:* the abbreviations used will be Mt for Matthew, Mk for Mark, and Lk for Luke. Everything is a direct quote of the gospel writers' quoting of Jesus. No quotation marks will be used except when Jesus quotes someone, as in a parable.)

Lk 2:49	Why were you searching for me? Did you not know that I must be in my Father's house?
Mt 5:13	You are the salt of the earth: but if salt has lost its taste, how can its saltiness be restored? (See also Lk 14:34.)
Mt 5:46-47	For if you love those who love you, what reward do you have? Do not even tax collectors do the same? And if you greet only your brothers and sisters, what are you doing more than others? Do not even the Gentiles do the same? (There is a similar list of questions in Lk 6:32-36, with one addition—If you lend to those from whom you hope to receive, what credit is that to you?)
Mt 6:25	Is not life more than food, and the body more than clothing?
Mt 6:26	Look at the birds of the air. . . . Are you not of more value than they?
Mt 6:27	And can any of you by worrying add a single hour to your span of life? (Also Lk 12:25.)
Mt 6:28,30	And why do you worry about clothing? Consider the lilies of the field, . . . Will he not much more clothe you—you of little faith? (In Lk 12:22-31, most of these are given as statements, rather than questions.)
Mt 7:3-4	Why do you see the speck in your neighbor's eye, but do not see the log in your own eye? Or how can you see to your neighbor, 'Let me take the speck out of your eye,' while the log is in your own eye? (Also Lk 6:41-42.)
Mt 7:9-10	Is there anyone among you who, if your child asks for bread will give a stone? Or if the child asks for a fish will give a snake? (Compare Lk 11:11-12.)

Mt 7:16	You will know them by their fruits. Are grapes gathered from thorns, or figs from thistles?
Lk 6:46	Why do you call me 'Lord, Lord,' and do not do what I tell you? (This is given as a statement in Mt 7:21.)
Mt 8:26	Why are you afraid, you of little faith?
Mk 2:8-9	Why do you raise such questions in your hearts? Which is easier, to say to the paralytic, 'Your sins are forgiven,' or to say, 'Stand up, and take your mat and walk'? (Compare Mt 9:4-5 and Lk 5:22-23.)
Mt 9:15	The wedding guests cannot mourn as long as the bridegroom is with them, can they? (Also Mk 2:19. Compare Lk 5:34.)
Mt 9:28	Do you believe I am able to do this?
Mt 10:29	Are not two sparrows sold for a penny? (In Lk 12:6 the question is, Are not five sparrows sold for two pennies?)
Mt 11:7-9	What did you go out into the wilderness to look at? A reed shaken by the wind? What then did you go out to see? Someone dressed in soft robes? . . . What then did you go out to see? A prophet? (Also Lk 7:24-26.)
Mt 11:16	But to what will I compare this generation? (Compare Lk 7:31.)
Mt 11:23	And you, Capernaum, will you be exalted to heaven? (Also Lk 10:15.)
Mt 12:3,5	Have you not read what David did when he and his companions were hungry? . . . Or have you not read in the law that on the sabbath the priests in the temple break the sabbath and yet are guiltless? (Compare Mk 2:25ff and Lk 6:3ff.)
Mk 3:4	Is it lawful to do good or to do harm on the sabbath, to save life or to kill? (Compare Lk 6:9. In Mt 12:10, unidentified persons ask Jesus a similar question, and he responds, Suppose one of you has only one sheep and it falls into a pit on the sabbath; will you not lay hold of it and lift it out? In a similar passage in Lk 14:5, Jesus asks, If one of you has a child or an ox that has fallen into a well, will you not immediately pull it out on a sabbath day?)
Lk 6:39	Can a blind person guide a blind person? Will not both fall into a pit? (A similar statement is given in Mt 15:14 as a statement.)
Lk 7:31	To what I will I compare the people of this generation, and what are they like?
Lk 7:42	(The question is about two debtors, one with a greater debt.) Now which of them will love him more?

Lk 7:44	Do you see this woman?
Mk 3:23	How can Satan cast out Satan? (In a parallel passage, Matthew includes the question, If Satan casts out Satan, he is divided against himself; how then will his kingdom stand? [Mt 12:26]. There is a similar question in Lk 11:18.)
Mt 12:27	If I cast out demons by Beelzebul, by whom do your own exorcists cast them out? (Also Lk 11:19.)
Mt 12:29	Or how can one enter a strong man's house and plunder his property, without first tying up the strong man? (Given as a statement in Mk 3:27 and in Lk 11:21-22.)
Mt 12:34	How can you speak good things, when you are evil?
Mk 3:33	Who are my mother and my brothers? (Also Mt 12:48, given as statement in Lk 8:21.)
Mk 4:13	Do you not understand this parable? Then how will you understand all the parables?
Mk 4:21	Is a lamp brought in to be put under the bushel basket, or under the bed and not on the lampstand? (Given as a statement in Lk 8:16.)
Mk 4:30	With what can we compare the kingdom of God, or what parable will we use for it? (Compare Lk 13:18.)
Mt 13:27-28	'Master did you not sow good seed in your field? Where, then did these weeds come from? . . . Then do you want us to go and gather them?' (These are questions by characters within a parable.)
Mt 13:51	Have you understood all this?
Mk 4:40	Why are you afraid? Have you still no faith? (Compare Mt 8:26 and Lk 8:25.)
Mk 5:9	What is your name? (Also Lk 8:30.)
Mk 5:31	Who touched my clothes? (Compare Lk 8:45. No question is included in Mt 9:21-22.)
Mk 5:39	Why do you make a commotion and weep?
Mk 6:38	How many loaves have you? (The event without questions is also recorded in Mt 14 and Lk 9.)
Mt 14:31	You of little faith, why did you doubt?
Mt 15:3	And why do you break the commandment of God for the sake of your tradition? (Here Jesus answers a question with a question.)
Mk 7:18-19	Then do you also fail to understand? Do you not see that whatever goes into a person from outside cannot defile, since it enters, not the heart but the stomach and goes out into the sewer? (Compare Mt 15:16-17.)

Mk 8:5	How many loaves do you have? (Also Mt 15:34. Here again, Jesus answers a question with a question.)
Mk 8:12	Why does this generation ask for a sign?
Mk 8:17-21	Why are you talking about having no bread? Do you still not perceive or understand? Are your hearts hardened? Do you have eyes, and fail to see? Do you have ears, and fail to hear? And do you not remember? When I broke the five loaves for the five thousand, how many baskets full of broken pieces did you collect? . . . And the seven for the four thousand, how many baskets full of broken pieces did you collect? . . . Do you not yet understand? (In Mt 16:8-12, Jesus asks a shorter series of questions, but then adds another, How could you fail to perceive that I was not speaking about bread?)
Mk 8:23	Can you see anything?
Mt 16:13,15	Who do people say that the Son of Man is? . . . But who do you say that I am? (Compare Mk 8:27-33 and Lk 9:18-22.)
Mk 9:16	What are you arguing about with them?
Mk 9:19	You faithless generation, how much longer must I be among you? How much longer must I put up with you? (Compare Mt 17:17 and Lk 9:41.)
Mk 9:21	How long has this been happening to him?
Mt 17:25	What do you think, Simon? From whom do kings of the earth take toll or tribute? From their children or from others?
Mk 9:33	What were you arguing about on the way?
Mt 18:12	What do you think? (In Lk 15:4, Jesus frames the whole parable in a question: Which one of you having a hundred sheep . . . finds it?)
Lk 10:26	What is written in the law? What do you read there? (In Mt 22:36-40 and Mk 12:28-31, the Pharisees ask Jesus about the greatest commandment, and he answers, much as the lawyer did to him in Lk 10.)
Lk 10:36	Which of these three, do you think, was a neighbor to the man who fell into the hands of the robbers?
*Lk 11:5-8	(In the RSV, this entire parable is framed as a question: Which of you who has a friend. . . ? In the NRSV, this parable begins: Suppose one of you has a friend . . . , and there is no question at the end.)

---

*Indicates exception to listing only the questions of Jesus translated by the NRSV version.

Lk 12:14	Friend, who set me to be a judge or arbitrator over you?
Lk 12:17,20	'What should I do for I have no place to store my crops?' 'You fool! This very night your life is being demanded of you. And the things you have prepared, whose will they be?'(Quotes of characters within a parable.)
Lk 12:42	Who then is the faithful and prudent manager whom his master will put in charge of his slaves, to give them their allowance of food at the proper time? (Compare Mt 24:45.)
Lk 12:51	Do you think that I have come to bring peace to the earth? (In Mt 10:34, Jesus gives this as a statement rather than a question. Indeed, in Lk, he immediately answers his own question.)
Lk 12:56	You hypocrites! You know how to interpret the appearance of earth and sky, but why do you not know how to interpret the present time?
Lk 12:57	And why do you not judge for yourselves what is right?
Lk 13:2,4	Do you think that because these Galileans suffered in this way they were worse sinners than all other Galileans? . . . Or those eighteen who were killed when the tower of Siloam fell on them—do you think that they were worse offenders than all others living in Jerusalem?
Lk 13:7	'Why should it be wasting the soil?' (Question by a character within a parable.)
Lk 13:15-16	You hypocrites! Does not each of you on the sabbath untie his ox or his donkey from the manger, and lead it away to give it water? And ought not this woman, a daughter of Abraham whom Satan bound for eighteen long years, be set free from this bondage on the sabbath day?
Lk 14:3,5	Is it lawful to cure people on the sabbath or not? If one of you has a child or an ox that has fallen into a well, will you not immediately pull it out on a sabbath day?
Lk 14:28,31	For which of you, intending to build a tower, does not first sit down and estimate the cost, to see whether he has enough to complete it? . . . Or what king, going out to wage war against another king, will not sit down first and consider whether he is able with ten thousand to oppose the one who comes against him with twenty thousand?
Lk 15:4,8	Which of you, having a hundred sheep . . . finds it? . . . Or what woman having ten silver coins . . . until she finds it?
Lk 16:11	If then you have not been faithful with the dishonest wealth, who will entrust to you the true riches? And if you have not been faithful with what belongs to another, who will give you what is your own?

Lk 17:7-9	Who among you would say to your slave who has just come in from plowing or tending sheep in the field, 'Come here at once and take your place at the table'? Would you not rather say to him, 'Prepare supper for me, put on your apron and serve me while I eat and drink; later you may eat and drink'? Do you thank the slave for doing what was commanded?
Lk 17:17-18	Were not ten made clean? But the other nine, where are they? Was none of them found to return and give praise to God except this foreigner?
Mk 10:3	What did Moses command you? (In Mt 19:4, Jesus offers a long question with quotes from the Torah within—Have you not read that the one who made them . . . one flesh?)
Mk 10:18	Why do you call me good? (Also Lk 18:19; compare Mt 19:17.)
Mt 20:6,13,15	'Why are you standing here idle all day?' . . . 'Friend, I am doing you no wrong; did you not agree with me for the usual daily wage? . . . Am I not allowed to do what I choose with what belongs to me? Or are you envious because I am generous?' (Questions by characters within a parable.)
Lk 18:7-8	And will not God grant justice to his chosen ones who cry to him day and night? Will he delay long in helping them? . . . And yet, when the Son of Man comes, will he find faith on earth?
Mk 10:36	What is it you want me to do for you? (Compare Mt 20:21.)
Mk 10:38	Are you able to drink the cup that I drink, or be baptized with the baptism that I am baptized with? (Compare Mt 20:22.)
Mk 10:51	What do you want me to do for you? (Also Mt 20:32 and Lk 19:41.)
Lk 19:22-23	'You knew, did you, that I was a harsh man, taking what I did not deposit and reaping why I did now sow? Why then did you not put my money into the bank?' (Questions by a character in a parable. Compare Mt 25:26.)
Mt 21:16	Yes; have you never read, 'Out of the mouths of infants and nursing babies you have prepared praise for yourself'?
Mk 11:17	Is it not written, 'My house shall be called a house of prayer for all nations'?
Mt 21:25	Did the baptism of John come from heaven, or was it of human origin? (Also Mk 11:30 and Lk 20:4.)

Mt 21:28,31	What do you think? ... Which of the two did the will of his father?
Lk 20:13,15,17	'What shall I do?' . . . What then will the owner or the vineyard do to them? What then does this text mean: 'The stone that the builders rejected has become the corner-stone'? (The first is a question by a character within the parable, the second and third are Jesus' questions at the end of the parable. See also Mt 21:33-46 and Mk 12:1-12.)
Mt 22:18,20	Why are you putting me to the test, you hypocrites? ... Whose head is this and whose title? (Also Mk 12:15-16; Compare Lk 20:23-24.)
Mk 12:24,26	Is not this the reason you are wrong, that you know neither the scriptures nor the power of God? . . . And as for the dead being raised, have you not read in the book of Moses, in the story about the bush, how God said to him, 'I am the God of Abraham, of Isaac, and the God of Jacob'? (Compare Mt 22:23-33 and Lk 20:27-40).
Mt 22:42,44,45	What do you think of the Messiah? Whose son is he? ... How is it then that David by the Spirit calls him Lord. . . ? If David thus calls him Lord, how can he be his son? (Compare Mk 12:35-37 and Lk 20:41-44).
Mt 23:17,19	You blind fools! For which is greater, the gold or the sanc-tuary that has made the gold sacred? . . . How blind you are! For which is greater, the gift or the altar that makes the gift sacred?
Mt 23:33	How can you escape being sentenced to hell?
Mk 13:2	Do you see these great buildings? (Compare Mt 24:1-3 and Lk 21:5-7.)
Mt 26:10	Why do you trouble the woman? (Compare Mk 14:6.)
Mk 14:14	Where is my guest room where I may eat the Passover with my disciples? (The question Jesus instructed his dis-ciples to ask a man carrying a jar of water, also Lk 22:11.)
Lk 22:27	For who is greater, the one who is at the table or the one who serves? Is it not the one at the table?
Lk 22:35	When I sent you out without a purse, bag, or sandals, did you lack anything?
Mk 14:37,41	Simon are you asleep? Could you not keep awake one hour? . . . Are you still sleeping and taking your rest? (Compare Mt 26:36-46 and Lk 22:40-46.)
*Mt 26:50	In the RSV, this verse reads, Friend, why are you here? In the NRSV it reads, Friend do what you are here to do.

---

*Indicates exception to listing only the questions of Jesus as translated by the NRSV.

Lk 22:48	Judas, is it with a kiss that you are betraying the Son of Man? (Only Luke includes this question in the account of Jesus' arrest, Mt 26:47-56 and Mk 14:43-52.)
Mt 26:53-54	Do you think that I cannot appeal to my Father, and he will at once send me more than twelve legions of angels? But how then would the scriptures be fulfilled, which say it must happen in this way?
Mk 14:48	Have you come out with swords and clubs to arrest me as though I were a bandit? (Also Mt 26:55 and Lk 22:52.)
Lk 23:31	For if they do this when the wood is green, what will happen when it is dry?
Mt 27:46	My God, My God, why have you forsaken me? (Also Mk 15:34.)
Lk 24:17	What are you discussing with each other while you walk along?
Lk 24:19	What things?
Lk 24:26	Was it not necessary that the Messiah should suffer these things and then enter into his glory?
Lk 24:38,41	Why are you frightened and why do doubts arise in your hearts? . . . Have you anything here to eat?

Appendix B

Jesus' Questions in the Gospel of John

1:38	What are you looking for?
1:50	Do you believe because I told you I saw you under the fig tree?
2:4	Woman, what concern is that to you and to me?
3:10	Are you a teacher of Israel, and yet you do not understand these things?
3:12	If I have told you about earthly things and you do not believe, how can you believe if I tell you about heavenly things?
4:35	Do you not say, 'Four months more, then comes the harvest'?
5:6	Do you want to be made well?
5:44	How can you believe when you accept glory from one another and do not seek the glory that comes from the one who alone is God?
5:47	But if you do not believe what he [Moses] wrote, how will you believe what I say?
6:5	Where are we to buy bread for these people to eat?
6:61-62	Does this offend you? Then what if you were to see the Son of Man ascending to where he was before?
6:67	Do you also wish to go away?
6:70	Did I not choose you, the twelve? Yet one of you is a devil.
7:19	Did not Moses give you the law? Yet none of you keeps the law. Why are you looking for an opportunity to kill me?
*7:28	In the RSV this verse is given: You know me, and you know where I come from? In the NRSV, the very same words are given as a statement.
8:10	Woman, where are they? Has no one condemned you?
8:25	Why do I speak to you at all?
8:43	Why do you not understand what I say?
8:46	Which of you convicts me of sin? If I tell the truth, why do you not believe me?
9:35	Do you believe in the Son of Man?

---

*Indicates exception to listing only the questions of Jesus as translated by the NRSV.

10:32	I have shown you many good works from the Father. For which of these are you going to stone me?
10:34	Is it not written in your law, 'I said, you are gods'?
11:9	Are there not twelve hours of daylight?
11:25b-26	Those who believe in me, even though they die, will live, and everyone who lives and believes in me will never die. Do you believe this?
11:34	Where have you laid him?
11:40	Did I not tell you that if you believed, you would see the glory of God?
12:27	Now my soul is troubled. And what should I say – 'Father, save me from this hour'? No, it is for this reason that I have come to this hour.
13:12	Do you know what I have done to you? (Jesus' question after washing the disciples' feet).
13:38	Will you lay down your life for me?
14:2	In my Father's house there are many dwelling places. If it were not so, would I have told you that I go to prepare a place for you?
14:9-10	Have I been with you all this time, Philip, and you still do not know me? Whoever has seen me has seen the Father. How can you say, 'Show us the Father'? Do you not believe that I am in the Father and the Father is in me?
16:19	Are you discussing among yourselves what I meant when I said, 'A little while, and you will no longer see me, and again a little while, and you will see me'?
16:31	Do you now believe?
18:4,7	Whom are you looking for?
18:11	Put your sword back into its sheath. Am I not to drink the cup that the Father has given me?
18:21	Why do you ask me? Ask those who heard what I said to them; they know what I said.
18:23	But if I have spoken rightly, why did you strike me?
18:34	Do you ask this on your own, or did others tell you about me?
20:15	Woman, why are you weeping? Whom are you looking for?
20:29	Have you believed because you have seen me? Blessed are those who have not seen and yet have come to believe.
21:5	Children, you have no fish have you?
21:15	Simon, son of John, do you love me more than these?
21:16	Simon, son of John, do you love me?
21:17	Simon, son of John, do you love me?
21:22	If it is my will that he remain until I come, what is that to you? Follow me!

Notes

Introduction

1. John Westerhoff (1976). *Will Our Children Have Faith?* New York: Seabury Press, p. 96, italics added.
2. Told by R. Benjamin Garrison in *Are You the Christ?* (1978). Nashville: Abingdon Press, p. 7.
3. Burton H. Throckmorton Jr. (1949, 1979). *Gospel Parallels: A Synopsis of the First Three Gospels.* New York: Thomas Nelson.
4. William Herzog II (1994). *Parables As Subversive Speech.* Louisville: Westminster/John Knox, p. 1.

Chapter 1

1. Chris Hedges (2002). *War Is a Force That Gives Life Meaning.* New York: Public Affairs Press, p. 3.
2. Quoted in Paul Welter (1987). *Counseling and the Search for Meaning.* Waco: Word Books, p. 53.
3. This is a brief summary of Frankl's concepts, taken primarily from two of his early books, *Man's Search for Meaning* (New York: Washington Square Press, Inc., 1959) and *The Will to Meaning* (New York: New American Library, 1969).
4. Joseph Fabry (1968). *The Pursuit of Meaning,* Boston: Beacon Press, 155, quoted in Welter, Counseling and the Search for Meaning, Waco: Word Books, 56.
5. Robert Leslie (1965). *Jesus and Logotherapy.* Nashville: Abingdon, p. 37.
6. Rowan Williams (2002). *Writing in the Dust.* Grand Rapids: Wm. B Eerdmans Publishing Company, p. 43.

Chapter 2

1. Carole Hyatt (1990). *Shifting Gears.* New York: Simon and Schuster, p. 23.
2. Jack Falvey (1987). *What's Next? Career Strategies After 35.* Charlotte: William Publishing, p. 26.
3. This and more such information is summarized in my book, *Midlife Journeys: A Traveler's Guide* (Cleveland: Pilgrim Press, 1996), pp. 82-84.
4. G. Lloyd Rediger (1997). *Clergy Killers: Guidance for Pastors and Congregations Under Attack.* Louisville: Westminster John Knox.
5. William Barclay (1958, 1975). The Gospel of Matthew. Volume 1. Philadelphia: The Westminster Press, p. 384.

6. By Elizabeth Chaney, quoted in Charles L. Allen (1953). *God's Psychiatry.* Westwood, NJ: Fleming H. Revell Company, a division of Baker Publishing Group p. 94. Reprinted with permission.

7. William Barclay *The Gospel of Luke.* Philadelphia: Westminster Press, p. 168.

8. Michael S. Northcott (1996). *The Environment and Christian Ethics.* Cambridge University Press, p. 74.

9. Helen Kromer and Frederick Silver (1961, 1963). *For Heaven's Sake.* Boston: Baker's Plays, pp. 21-23. Reprinted with permission.

10. Tom Brokaw (1998). *The Greatest Generation.* New York: Random House, Bookjacket. In turn he is quoting, summarizing, and paraphrasing his opening chapter, particularly xix-xx.

11. Quoted in Richard Bolles (1978). *The Three Boxes of Life.* Berkeley: Ten Speed Press, p. 325.

Chapter 3

1. Quoted in Richard P. Olson and Joe H. Leonard Jr. (1990). *Ministry with Families in Flux.* Louisville: Westminster John Knox, p. 9.

2. Mary Pipher (1996). *The Shelter of Each Other.* New York: A Grossett/Putnam Book, pp. 9-10. In more ways than these endnotes can show, I am indebted to Mary Pipher for the discussion in this chapter.

3. Ibid, p. 11.

4. Ibid, p. 14.

5. Ibid, p. 15.

6. CDC (2002). Trends in Cigarette Smoking Among High School Students - United States 1991-2001. *Morbidity and Mortality Weekly Report,* May 17.

7. Nick Stinett and John De Frain (1985). *The Secrets of Strong Families.* Boston: Little Brown.

8. Pipher, *Shelter,* p. 231.

9. Ibid, pp. 251-252.

10. Ibid, p. 23.

11. Gilbert Meilaender (2001). "After September 11." *Christian Century,* September 26-October 3, p. 8.

Chapter 4

1. Gaylord Noyce (1989). *The Minister As Moral Counselor.* Nashville: Abingdon, p. 41.

2. G. Lloyd Rediger (1997). *Clergy Killers: Guidance for Pastors and Congregations Under Attack.* Louisville: Westminster John Knox, p. 13. He is reporting a 1996 survey of Protestant clergy by *Leadership* magazine.

3. Bruce Bawer (1997). *Stealing Jesus: How Fundamentalism Betrays Christianity.* New York: Crown Publishers.

Chapter 5

1. Howard Stone (1991). "Depression." In *Handbook for Basic Types of Pastoral Care and Counseling* (pp. 172-173), Howard W. Stone and William M. Clements (eds.). Nashville: Abingdon. Use by permission.
2. Ibid, p. 173.
3. Richard O'Connor (1997). *Undoing Depression.* Boston: Little, Brown, and Company, p. 17.
4. Ibid, pp. 21, 31.
5. *What Everyone Should Know About Depression.* A Scriptographic Product. South Deerfield, MA: Channing L. Bete, Co., Inc., pp. 8-9.
6. Quoted by Rev. Dr. Rodney Romney in *The Spire,* newsletter for Seattle First Baptist Church, Vol. 58, No. 19, October 1, 1997.
7. O'Connor, *Undoing Depression,* pp. 25-26.

Chapter 6

1. Ayah M. Pines and Elliot Arson with Ditz Quivery (1981). *Burnout: From Tedium to Personal Growth.* New York: The Free Press, pp. 4-5.
2. Wade Clark Roof (1993). *A Generation of Seekers: Religion and the Baby Boomer Population.* San Francisco: Harper.
3. Pines and Arson, *Burnout,* p. 18.
4. Ibid, p. 19.
5. Quoted in Ernest Campbell (1974). *Locker in a Room with Open Doors.* Waco: Word Books, p. 117.
6. Lloyd Rediger (1982). *Coping with Clergy Burnout.* Valley Forge: Judson Press.
7. Gary Reiff (1989). Newsletter of First Baptist Church of Peoria, Illinois, June 7.

Chapter 7

1. Anne Lamott (1999). *Traveling Mercies: Some Thoughts on Faith.* New York: Pantheon Books, p. 48.
2. Ibid.
3. "God's Presence in Each of Us." *The Living Pulpit,* Volume 1, no. 3, July-September, 1992, p. 11.
4. Lamott, *Traveling Mercies,* p. 255.
5. Quoted by Joan Delaplane, O.P. (1992). "That Two Lettered Word." In *The Living Pulpit,* Vol. 1, No. 3, July-September, p. 13.
6. Quoted in Alan Walker (1962). *The Many Sided Cross of Jesus.* Nashville: Abingdon Press, p. 31.
7. "God's Presence in Each of Us," p. 28.
8. C. E. B. Cranfield (1951). "Love, Lover, Love Beloved." In Alan Richardson (Ed.), *A Theological Word Book of the Bible.* New York: The Macmillan Company, p. 134.

Chapter 8

1. Elton Trueblood (1965). *The Lord's Prayers.* New York: Harper and Row, p. 13.

2.Thomas Keating (1995). *Contemplative Prayer.* (Audiotape). Boulder, CO: Sounds True.

3. John Casteel (1955). *Rediscovering Prayer.* New York: Association Press, p. 13.

4. Barry Ulanov and Ann Ulanov (1982). *Primary Speech: A Psychology of Prayer.* Atlanta: John Knox Press.

5. Richard Foster (1992). *Prayer: Finding the Heart's True Home.* San Francisco: HarperSanFrancisco, p. 3.

6. These quotes come from a variety of sources. The last four are from Olive Wyon (1963). *The School of Prayer.* New York: The Macmillan Company, pp. 5, 17. Wyon's own quote is in turn a paraphrase of sixteenth century writer Bellarmin.

7. Trueblood, *The Lord's Prayers,* p. 14.

8. Richard Rohr (1999). *Everything Belongs: The Gift of Contemplative Prayer.* New York: Crossroad Publishing Company, p. 39.

9. Quoted in Foster, *Prayer: Finding,* p. 63. It comes from Nouwen, H. (1981). *Making All Things New.* San Francisco: Harper and Row, p. 69.

10. Rohr, *Everything,* p. 31.

11. This is listed as a "Traditional Folk Song" in *The Hymnal for Worship and Celebration,* Tom Fettke, senior editor (Waco: Word Music, 1986).

12. The "Please Touch" story and the words from this hymn are quoted in *Seven Questions Jesus Asked* by R. Benjamin Garrison (Nashville: Abingdon, 1975), p. 23.

13. Foster, *Prayer: Finding,* p. 49.

Chapter 9

1. Quoted in George Buttrick (1952). *Prayer.* New York: Abingdon-Cokesbury, pp. 79-80.

2. Quoted in Lloyd John Ogilvie (1983). *Praying with Power.* Ventura, CA: Regal Books, p. 77.

3. Larry Dossey (1997). "Prayer Is Good Medicine." *The Saturday Evening Post,* November/December, pp. 52-55, 82. See also Dr. Dossey's *Healing Words: The Power of Prayer and the Practice of Medicine.* New York: Harper Paperbacks.

4. Charles F. Stanley (1982). *Handle with Prayer.* Wheaton: Victor Books, pp. 67, 68.

5. Buttrick, *Prayer,* p. 114.

6. Ogilvie, *Praying with Power,* p. 80.

7. Harry Emerson Fosdick (1949). *The Meaning of Prayer.* New York: Association Press, p. 125.

8. Cynthia Pearl Maus (Ed.) (1938). *Christ and the Fine Arts.* New York: Harper and Row, p. 681.

9. Fosdick, *The Meaning of Prayer,* pp. 130-131.

Chapter 10

1. Rowan Williams (2002). *Writing in the Dust: After September 11.* Grand Rapids: Wm. B. Eerdmans Publishing Co., pp. 7-8.
2. C. S. Lewis (1961). *A Grief Observed.* (Seabury Press, pp. 25, 27, quoted in Kenneth R. Mitchell and Herbert Anderson (1983). *All Our Losses, All Our Griefs.* Louisville: The Westminster Press, p. 79.
3. Jeffry R. Zurheide (1997). *When Faith is Tested: Pastoral Responses to Suffering and Tragic Death.* Minneapolis: Fortress, pp. 14-17.
4. Ibid, pp. 19-24.
5. Source unknown. I have heard this limerick and repeated it for years and years.
6. Harold S. Kushner (1981). *When Bad Things Happen to Good People.* New York: Schocken Books.
7. Zurheide, *When Faith Is Tested,* pp. 26-34.
8. Leslie Weatherhead (1954). *The Will of God.* New York: Abingdon Press, p. 12.
9. Ibid, p. 20.
10. James Stalker, quoted in R. Benjamin Garrison (1975). *Seven Questions Jesus Asked.* New York: Abingdon, p. 72.
11. Barbara Brown Taylor (1998). *God in Pain: Teaching Sermons on Suffering.* Nashville: Abingdon, p. 112. Used by permission.
12. Ibid, p. 114.
13. Leslie Weatherhead (1962). *Salute to a Sufferer.* New York: Abingdon Press, p. 21.
14. Taylor, *God in Pain,* pp. 122-123.
15. Quoted in Weatherhead, *Salute,* p. 22.

Chapter 11

1. Both these statements come from Andrew D. Lester (1995). *Hope in Pastoral Care and Counseling.* Louisville: Westminster John Knox, p. 59. This fine book richly informs me as I pursue this important question.
2. Quoted in Lester, *Hope,* p. 60. The quote is from Erikson's book, *Insight and Responsibility,* New York: W. W. Norton, p. 115.
3. Ibid, pp. 55-56.
4. Ibid, p. 73.
5. Paul Zahl (1992). "Preaching Hope As Retrospective: An Evangelical View." In *The Living Pulpit,* Vol. 1, No. 1, January-March, p. 11.
6. Lester, *Hope,* pp. 63-65.
7. "Quotes on the Many Meanings of Hope." *The Living Pulpit,* Vol. 1, No. 1, p. 26.
8. William Barclay (1958). *More New Testament Words.* New York: Harper and Brothers, p. 46.
9. Lynch is cited in John R Donahue, S.J. (1992). "Parables As Images of Hope." in *The Living Pulpit,* Vol. 1, No. 1, January-March p. 12. The quote was from Kenner's book, *The Pound Era,* Berkely: University of California Press, p. 39.

10. Joan Delaplane, O.P. (1992). "A Future of Hope." In *The Living Pulpit,* Vol. 1, No. 1, January-March, p. 15.

Chapter 12

1. Richard P. Olson and Joe H. Leonard Jr. (1996). *A New Day for Family Ministry.* Bethesda, MD: The Alban Institute pp. 8-10.
2. Barbara Brown Taylor (1998). "Escape from the Tomb." *Christian Century,* April 1, Vol. 115, No. 10, p. 339.
3. James P. Berkely (1958). *Reading the Gospel of John.* Valley Forge: Judson Press, p. 223.
4. Frederick Buechner (1979). *Peculiar Treasures: A Biblical Who's Who.* San Francisco: Harper and Row, pp. 102-103.
5. As I mentioned in the introduction, New Testament scholar David May has pointed out that Jesus' words to Mary in John 20:17 might be yet another question, "have I not ascended? . . ." and this reading might aid in the interpretation of this passage.
6. Buechner, *Peculiar Treasures,* p. 103.
7. Taylor, "Escape," p. 339.
8. Ibid.
9. Ibid.
10. R. Benjamin Garrison (1975). *Seven Questions Jesus Asked.* Nashville: Abingdon, p. 84.
11. Barbara Brown Taylor (1988). *God in Pain: Teaching Sermons on Suffering.* Nashville: Abingdon, p. 68. Used by permission.
12. Raymond Moody (1976). *Life After Life.* New York: Bantam Books.
13. Roger Lovette (1986). *Questions Jesus Raised.* Nashville: Broadman, pp. 81-82.

Epilogue

1. Rowan Williams (2002). *Writing in the Dust.* Grand Rapids: Wm. B. Eerdmans Publishing, p. 9.
2. Ronald Stone (1999). *The Ultimate Imperative: An Interpretation of Christian Ethic.* Cleveland: Pilgrim Press, p. 98.
3. This summary is taken from: Bruce Larson (1978). *The Whole Christian.* Waco: Word Books, pp. 51-52.

Bibliography

Allen, Charles (1953). *God's Psychiatry*. Westwood, NJ: Fleming H. Revell Company.

Barclay, William (1953). *The Gospel of Luke*. Philadelphia: Westminster Press.

Barclay, William (1958). *More New Testament Words*. New York: Harper and Brothers.

Barclay, William (1958, 1975). *The Gospel of Matthew, Volume I*. Philadelphia: The Westminster Press.

Bass, Dorothy (2000). *Receiving the Day: Christian Practices for Opening the Gift of Time*. San Francisco: Jossey-Bass.

Bawer, Bruce (1997). *Stealing Jesus: How Fundamentalism Betrays Christianity*. New York: Crown Publishers.

Berger, Peter (1997). *Redeeming Laughter: The Comic Dimension of Human Experience*. New York: Walter De Gruyter.

Berkely, James P. (1958). *Reading the Gospel of John*. Valley Forge: Judson Press.

Bolles, Richard (1978). *The Three Boxes of Life*. Berkeley: Ten Speed Press.

Bolles, Richard (2004). *What Color Is Your Parachute?* Berkeley: Ten Speed Press, revised edition each year.

Brokaw, Tom (1998). *The Greatest Generation*. New York: Random House.

Buechner, Frederick (1979). *Peculiar Treasures: A Biblical Who's Who*. San Francisco: Harper and Row.

Buttrick, George (1952). *Prayer*. New York: Abingdon-Cokesbury.

Casteel, John L. (1955). *Rediscovering Prayer*. New York: Association Press.

CDC (2002). Trends in Cigarette Smoking Among High School Students - United States 1991-2001. *Morbidity and Mortality Weekly Report*. Centers for Disease Control and Prevention, May 17.

Clinebell, Howard (1966, 1984). *Basic Types of Pastoral Counseling*. Nashville: Abingdon Press.

Cranfield, C.E.B. (1951). "Love, Lover, Lovely, Beloved." In Richardson, Alan (Ed.), *A Theological Wordbook of the Bible* (pp. 131-136). New York: The Macmillan Company.

De Frain, John and Nick Stinett (1985). *Secrets of Strong Families*. Boston: Little Brown.

Delaplane, Joan, O.P. (1992a). "A Future Full of Hope." *The Living Pulpit,* January-March, 1(1): 14-16.

Delaplane, Joan, O.P. (1992b). "That Two Lettered Word." In *The Living Pulpit,* July-September. 1(1): 12-13.

Donahue, John R., S.J. (1992). "Parables As Images of Hope." In *The Living Pulpit,* Vol. 1, No. 1, January-March.

Dossey, Larry (1993). *Healing Words.* New York: HarperPaperbacks.

Dossey, Larry (1997). "Prayer Is Good Medicine." *The Saturday Evening Post,* November/December. pp. 52-55, 82.

Erikson, Erik (1964). *Insight and Responsibility.* New York: W. W. Norton.

Falvey, Jack (1987). *What's Next? Career Strategies After 35.* Charlotte, NC: Williamson Publishing.

Fosdick, Harry Emerson (1915). *The Meaning of Prayer.* New York: Association Press.

Foster, Richard (1992). *Prayer: Finding Your Heart's True Home.* San Francisco: HarperSanFrancisco.

Frankl, Viktor (1959). *Man's Search for Meaning.* New York: Washington Square Press, Inc.

Frankl, Viktor (1969). *The Will to Meaning.* New York: New American Library.

Gallagher, Nora (1998). *Things Seen and Unseen: A Year Lived in Faith.* New York: Vintage Books.

Garrison, R. Benjamin (1975). *Seven Questions Jesus Asked.* Nashville: Abingdon Press.

Garrison, R. Benjamin (1978). *Are You the Christ?* Nashville: Abingdon Press.

Hedges, Chris (2002). *War Is a Force That Gives Life Meaning.* New York: Public Affairs Press.

Herzog, William, II (1994). *Parables As Subversive Speech.* Louisville: Westminster John Knox.

Hyatt, Carole (1990). Shifting Gears. New York: Simon and Schuster.

Jones, Kirk (2001). *Rest in the Storm.* Valley Forge: Judson Press.

Keating, Thomas (1995). *Contemplative Prayer.* (An audiotape). Boulder, CO: Sounds True.

Kornfeld, Margaret (2000). *Cultivating Wholeness: A Guide to Care and Counseling in the Faith Communities.* New York: Continuum.

Kromer, Helen and Frederick Silver (1961, 1963). *For Heaven's Sake.* Boston: Baker's Plays.

Kushner, Harold S. (1981). *When Bad Things Happen to Good People.* New York: Schocken Books.

Lamott, Anne (1999). *Traveling Mercies: Some Thoughts on Faith.* New York: Pantheon Books.

Leslie, Robert (1965). *Jesus and Logotherapy.* Nashville: Abingdon Press.

Lester, Andrew (1995). *Hope in Pastoral Care and Counseling.* Louisville: Westminster John Knox.

Lewis, C.S. (1961). *A Grief Observed.* New York: Seabury Press.

Lovette, Roger (1986). *Questions Jesus Raised.* Nashville: Baptist Sunday School Board.

Maus, Cynthia Pearl (Ed.) (1938). *Christ and the Fine Arts.* New York: Harper and Row.

McBride, J. LeBron (1998). *Spiritual Crisis: Surviving Trauma to the Soul.* Binghamton, NY: The Haworth Press.

Milaender, Gilbert (2001). "After September 11." *Christian Century,* September 26-October 3, 8.

Mitchell, Kenneth and Herbert Anderson (1983). *All Our Losses, All Our Griefs.* Louisville: Westminster John Knox.

Moody, Raymond (1976). *Life After Life.* New York: Bantam Books.

Northcott, Michael S. (1996). *The Environment and Christian Ethics.* Cambridge: University Press.

Nouwen, Henri (1981). *Making All Things New.* San Francisco: Harper and Row.

Nouwen, Henri J.M. (1982). *A Letter of Consolation.* San Francisco: Harper and Row.

Nouwen, Henri J.M. (1994). *Life of the Beloved: Spiritual Living in a Secular World.* New York: Crossroad.

Noyce, Gaylord (1989). *The Minister As Moral Counselor.* Nashville: Abingdon Press.

O'Connor, Richard (1997). *Undoing Depression.* Boston: Little, Brown, and Company.

Ogilvie, Lloyd John (1983). *Praying with Power.* Ventura, CA: Regal Books.

Olson, Richard P. (1996). *Midlife Journeys: A Traveler's Guide.* Cleveland: Pilgrim Press.

Olson, Richard P. (1998). *A Different Kind of Man.* Valley Forge: Judson.

Olson, Richard P. and Joe H. Leonard (1990). *Ministry with Families in Flux.* Louisville: Westminster John Knox.

Olson, Richard P. and Joe H. Leonard (1996). *A New Day for Family Ministry.* Bethesda, MD: The Alban Institute.

Pines, Ayah M. and Elliot Arson with Ditz Quivery (1981). *Burnout: From Tedium to Personal Growth.* New York: The Free Press.

Pipher, Mary (1996). *The Shelter of Each Other.* New York: A Grossett/Putnam Book.

Rediger, G. Lloyd (1982). *Coping with Clergy Burnout.* Valley Forge: Judson Press.

Rediger, G. Lloyd (1997). *Clergy Killers: Guidance for Pastors and Congregations Under Attack.* Louisville: Westminster John Knox.

Rediger, G. Lloyd (2000). *Fit to Be Pastor.* Louisville: Westminster John Knox.

Rohr, Richard (1999, 2003). *Everything Belongs: The Gift of Contemplative Prayer.* New York: Crossroad Publishing Company.

Roof, Wade Clark (1993). *A Generation of Seekers: Religion and the Baby Boomer Population.* San Francisco: HarperSanFrancisco.

Stanley, Charles F. (1982). *Handle with Prayer.* Wheaton: Victor Books.

Stone, Howard W. (1991). "Depression." In Stone, Howard W. and William M. Clements (Eds.) *Handbook for Basic Types of Pastoral Care and Counseling.* (pp. 172-208). Nashville: Abingdon Press.

Styron, William (1990). *Darkness Visible: A Memoir of Madness.* New York: Vintage Books.

Taylor, Barbara Brown (1998). "Escape from the Tomb." *Christian Century,* April 1, 39.

Taylor, Barbara Brown (1998). *God in Pain: Teaching Sermons on Suffering.* Nashville: Abingdon Press.

Throckmorton, Burton H., Jr. (1949, 1979). *Gospel Parallels: A Synopsis of the First Three Gospels.* New York: Thomas Nelson.

Trueblood, Elton (1965). *The Lord's Prayers.* New York: Harper and Row.

Ulanov, Barry and Ann Ulanov (1982). *Primary Speech: A Psychology of Prayer* Atlanta: John Knox Press.

Walker, Alan (1962). *The Many Sided Cross of Jesus.* Nashville: Abingdon Press.

Weatherhead, Leslie (1954). *The Will of God.* New York: Abingdon Press.

Weatherhead, Leslie (1962). *Salute to a Sufferer.* New York: Abingdon Press.

Welter, Paul (1987). *Counseling and the Search for Meaning.* Waco: Word Books.

Westerhoff, John (1976). *Will Our Children Have Faith?* New York: Seabury Press.

What Everyone Should Know About Depression (n.d.). A Scriptographic Product. South Deerfield, MA: Channing L. Bete, Co. Inc.

Williams, Rowan (2002). *Writing in the Dust.* Grand Rapids: Wm. B. Eerdmans Publishing Company.

Wyon, Olive (1963). *The School of Prayer.* New York: The MacMillan Company.

Zahl, Paul (1992). "Preaching Hope As Retrospective: An Evangelical View." In *The Living Pulpit,* January-March. 1(1): 10-11.

Zurheide, Jeffrey R. (1997). *When Faith Is Tested: Pastoral Responses to Suffering and Tragic Death.* Minneapolis: Fortress Press.

Index